Investor Stewardship and the UK Stewardship Code

Daniel Cash · Robert Goddard

Investor Stewardship and the UK Stewardship Code

The Role of Institutional Investors in Corporate Governance

palgrave
macmillan

Daniel Cash
Aston University
Birmingham, UK

Robert Goddard
Aston University
Birmingham, UK

ISBN 978-3-030-87151-2 ISBN 978-3-030-87152-9 (eBook)
https://doi.org/10.1007/978-3-030-87152-9

This Palgrave Macmillan imprint is published by the registered company Springer Nature Switzerland AG
The registered company address is: Gewerbestrasse 11, 6330 Cham, Switzerland

Contents

1 **Introduction** 1

2 **The UK Stewardship Code 2010 as a Response to the Financial Crisis** 5
2.1 Introduction 5
2.2 Milestones to the First-Ever 'Stewardship Code' 7
2.3 The Walker Review 9
2.4 The Dreaded Task of Implementation 11
2.5 Conclusion 14

3 **A Decade of Development** 19
3.1 Introduction 19
3.2 Main Criticisms of the First Codes 20
3.2.1 The Issue of Fiduciary Duty 22
3.2.2 Asset Owners and Managers: The Need for Alignment 23
3.2.3 The Realities of the Implementation of a Stewardship Code 24
3.3 The Kingman Review 25
3.3.1 International Impact 29
3.4 Conclusion 31

4 **The Stewardship Code 2020** 37
4.1 Introduction 37
4.2 The New Code 38

4.2.1 *A New Set of Principles* 40
4.2.2 *Differences from the 2012 Stewardship Code* 42
4.2.3 *Major Issues That Have Already Been Revealed* 45
4.3 *Early Signs* 47
4.4 *Conclusion* 49

5 The Future of Stewardship 53
5.1 *Introduction* 53
5.2 *The Fiduciary Disconnect* 54
5.2.1 *Way Forward* 57
5.3 *The Importance (and Risk) of Assurance* 58
5.4 *ARGA* 62
5.5 *Regulatory Alignment and Institutional Investors* 65
5.6 *Conclusion* 68

6 Conclusion 73

Index 77

CHAPTER 1

Introduction

> Effective and sustainable shareholder engagement is one of the cornerstones of the corporate governance model of listed companies, which depends on checks and balances between the different organs and different stakeholders. Greater involvement of shareholders in corporate governance is one of the levers that can help improve the financial and non-financial performance of companies, including as regards environmental, social, and governance factors…[1]

The term 'stewardship' can mean different things in different contexts. More generally, the concept relates to certain characteristics like long-term thinking, care, consciousness, purpose, and contribution.[2] It is almost thirty years since the Committee chaired by Sir Adrian Cadbury said almost the same thing as the quote leading this introduction: 'given the weight of their votes, the way in which institutional shareholders use their power to influence the standards of corporate governance is of fundamental performance'.[3] Therefore, in this book, we focus on the financial arena and the attachment of the concept of stewardship to the act of engagement from 'institutional investors' with the companies that they invest in. This is not an entirely new phenomena, but it is central to the modern business environment and has grown to become 'mainstream'. With the changing nature of the economic environment over recent decades, and the structural constitution of how capital moves around the financial system, the focus is now on making systemically important

D. Cash and R. Goddard, *Investor Stewardship and the UK Stewardship Code*, https://doi.org/10.1007/978-3-030-87152-9_1

investors both more responsible, and also key watchdogs over the financial system. Yet, we question throughout the model of involving shareholders more and whether the need to encourage is a sign that, ultimately, it is not achievable.

With regard to the financial arena and the role played by institutional investors specifically, the concept of engagement by these shareholders has long been acknowledged and encouraged.[4] It is worth noting here, very briefly, that the term 'institutional investor' is a 'catch-all' term that in reality describes a diverse set of organised and 'sophisticated' investors. We shall look at these complexities in much more detail as we go through, because that diversity is critically important with regard to understanding both the potential success of any 'Code' seeking to encourage stewardship and engagement, and also the potential limitations to any Code. For the uninitiated, there is a simple (but very crude) way of understanding the 'institutional investor' moniker. We can think of the term as encompassing two particular 'classes': asset owners, and asset managers. An example of an asset owner could be a pension fund, who collect the pension contributions of employees or savers, and seek to build the pot so that the value increases to meet the demands of the pension holders throughout the lifetime of the fund. Asset owners can and do invest those funds themselves, but they also often employ others to do it for them, which can be relatively cheaper than conducting the analysis and paying for investment services. Those organisations are called asset managers, and exist to invest others' monies, usually from within an 'investment mandate' that is set by the asset owner. There are, naturally, complications with this crude dualised understanding. For instance, organisations may be employed to conduct stewardship activities for the asset owner; for example, proxy voting organisations will conduct voting responsibilities on one's behalf, for a fee. The underlying sentiment to all of this is cost efficiency.

To return, there has been a traditional understanding of investor-based stewardship in that investors, once invested in an entity, will monitor the performance of that entity, exercise the rights associated with their shareholding, engage with the management of the company, and generally seek to provide an internal oversight position within the confines of the legally created corporate structure. That is the *theorised* model, when in reality an institutional investor will usually 'walk' away from an investment rather than voice their concerns etc., again under the umbrella of cost efficiency. If there is cause to do so, the concept of investor stewardship can entail more direct and impactful action, with an example being the coordination of other shareholders to force through a particular action within the company (say, voting to change remuneration policies, for example). This role has been steadily increasing in importance over the past 50 years as the landscape of what an investor is has rapidly changed. Although the trend is not universal—as some cultures have adapted differently to the changing financial and technological landscape—some countries have seen a tremendous shift in their investor make up. In the UK for example, the proportion of household assets held by pension funds, insurance companies, mutual funds and other institutional investors increased from 36% in 1995 to 44% in 2005.[5] This concentration has declined somewhat in recent years (particularly from pension funds),[6] but the analysis of the picture in 2005 is relevant because of what was to happen two years later.

The Financial Crisis was a generation-defining moment that caused several investigations from around the world to conclude that more needed to be done. One element amongst many that was revealed was that the new investor environment, particularly in the UK and the US, involved a number of inherent dynamics that lent itself to a lack of monitoring and engagement within some of the world's largest and societally important companies. With the distance between the investor (by which we mean 'retail' investor or those that invest in much larger investing vehicles) or saver (for pension funds) and the company growing ever wider—and in truth the distance between the institutional investor and the company itself growing ever wider because of the rise of financial intermediaries— it became clear that this particular investor dynamic had spun out of control. The incentives to monitor, and to push for longer-term strategies, were outweighed by many other factors that all concluded with a system centred in short-term thinking, yield chasing, and disintermediation. The rise of 'investor capitalism'[7] coincided with one of the most impact financial collapses in human history, and the result was catastrophic and is still being felt heavily today.

In response to these developments, a number of initiatives and ideas were actioned. One of them, which is the focus of this book, was to develop specific codes of practice for investors so that the stewardship role that many thought the investor ought to play, was systemically realised. Our focus is on the development of the UK Stewardship Code and its iterations. The development and rationale of each, the successes and limitations of the Code, as well as the future for the concept of stewardship in the UK (and beyond, given its primacy in influencing other jurisdictions) will all be assessed. Our aim is to ultimately provide you, the reader, with a focused insight into this concept of stewardship and the development of the new UK Stewardship Code 2020. What we will see is a story of political strife and intrigue, a societal response to a societal crisis, but most of all a picture of a *system* that is far from perfect. That systemic picture will be referred to throughout because the concept of investors actively engaging with the companies they invest in, and ultimately holding them to account, is of the utmost importance for economic and societal progression.

Notes

1. Directive (EU) 2017/828—Preamble (14).
2. Didier Cossin and Ong Boon Hwee, *Inspiring Stewardship* (John Wiley and Sons 2016) 4.
3. The Committee on the Financial Aspects of Corporate Governance, *Report of the Committee on the Financial Aspects of Corporate Governance* (1992) https://ecgi.global/sites/default/files//codes/documents/cadbury.pdf, 6.10.
4. Lee Roach, 'The UK Stewardship Code' (2011) 11 *Journal of Corporate Law Studies* 2 464, 463–93.
5. Peter Butler and Simon Wong, 'Recent Trends in Institutional Investor Responsibilities and Stewardship' (2011) 16 *Pensions* 80–5.
6. Office for National Statistics, 'Ownership of UK Quoted Shares: 2018' (2020) https://www.ons.gov.uk/economy/investmentspensionsandtrusts/bulletins/ownershipofukquotedshares/2018 (accessed 19 June 2021).
7. Alexander Styhre, *Corporate Governance, the Firm and Investor Capitalism: Legal-Political and Economic Views* (Edward Elgar 2016).

CHAPTER 2

The UK Stewardship Code 2010 as a Response to the Financial Crisis

2.1 Introduction

The Financial Crisis of 2007–2008, and the aftereffects of the generation-defining event became a pinch-point for re-evaluation on many fronts. In terms of the financial sector, Tan makes the valid point that 'the financial crisis thus compels us to re-examine current Anglo-American paradigms of corporate governance', and particularly on two fronts: the 'ends' of corporate governance i.e. what the purpose of corporate governance is and to whose interest should a company be governed, and then the 'means' of corporate governance i.e. are current corporate governance infrastructures adequate?[1] After the height of the Financial Crisis, it was understandably noted that the topic of corporate governance and the role of particular sectors within the corporate governance framework was high on the agenda and became 'one of the most debated issues' in the wake of the financial collapse.[2]

Whilst banks, insurers, credit rating agencies, mortgage developers, and many other financial sectors came in for massive criticism, investors were particularly highlighted for being one of the contributing causes of the crash because:

> [Institutional shareholders] have tended to be reactive rather than proactive and seldom challenge boards in sufficient number to make a difference...

D. Cash and R. Goddard, *Investor Stewardship and the UK Stewardship Code*, https://doi.org/10.1007/978-3-030-87152-9_2

in some instances shareholders have been equally concerned with short-termism as have manager and traders, neglecting the effect of excessive risk taking.[3]

Butler and Wong add to the OECD's understanding above that the institutional investors who hold the shares of these systemically important companies had simply 'failed to discharge the obligations expected of them'.[4] Whilst there are reasons for why the investors may have taken the actions that they did, the criticism in the aftermath was unwavering. A Treasury Select Committee in the UK concluded that 'institutional investors have failed in one of their core tasks, namely the effective scrutiny and monitoring the decisions of boards and executive management in the banking sector, and hold[ing] them accountable for their performance'. Ultimately, Lord Myners neatly summed up the sentiment by declaring institutional investors as being 'absentee landlords'.[5] We may need to be careful with this concept of modern shareholders being 'landlords' though because it has been identified that the average shareholding, on a global scene, is less than 6 months.[6] The reason for this could lie in the development that 'shareholding', as a concept, has changed dramatically in the modern era. Now, arguably, shares are merely components to be used in a global trading game, rather than investments in the fortunes of companies.[7] Such short time horizons for the holding of shares simply does not translate to the increasing of care, in fact it is the opposite. This is important to remember.

There is a concept that underpins everything that this book will cover—trust. In the aftermath of the Financial Crisis, any trust in the financial sector to refrain from exploiting their trusted and societally centralised position was 'eroded'.[8] Therefore, one of the primary aims of post-Crisis regulatory initiatives was to restore confidence in the financial sector and its ability to simultaneously think about others and the wider picture, rather than just themselves and profit above all else. It is on that basis that the concept of investor stewardship was reawakened and calls for a new and structured approach to investors taking responsibility were uttered.

Before we get into what was done, some context is needed. If we were to say to you 'why would an investor want to monitor the management and control of the company they are invested in?' the answer should be quite obvious; an investor should want to monitor and engage with the company they are invested in because they want to ensure that their investment is both safe, and that they will see a healthy return on that investment. This makes sense. However, what if that investor held investments in tens, hundreds, or even thousands of companies? What if, by design, their investment portfolio was incredibly diversified so that they were not overinvested in any particular sector? Would it still make sense to monitor *every* company's management that they are invested in? Such monitoring takes time, and that time is money. If one was to balance out all of the costs and time involved in meeting such 'obligations' as we heard of earlier, would it not just be easier and more efficient to 'walk'? Rather than engage and attempt to change decisions and/or behaviours in the company, would it not simply be most cost-efficient to display one's displeasure by selling one's shares and moving on? This, in a very crude nutshell, is the investment dynamic that has developed with the rise of the institutional investor and the modern form of capitalism. Diversification is highly efficient, but majoritively for *that particular investor*; for the system, it creates particular difficulties which, when duplicated on a large scale, can result in systemic failure.

On that basis then, it was argued after the Financial Crisis that society cannot simply rely on investors to 'do the right thing' because, quite frankly, there is no one 'right thing' in this context. Therefore, in a Report commissioned by the UK Government after the Financial Crisis, Sir David Walker outlined a number of issues and potential ways forward for the sector. Whilst the development to the most current 'Stewardship Code' in the UK has been laid out in the literature, it is worth revisiting to clarify the particular milestones that have led us to the Stewardship Code 2020.

2.2 Milestones to the First-Ever 'Stewardship Code'

It is tempting to start with the 'Walker Review' led by Sir David Walker, as it expressly called for the development of a purpose-built Stewardship Code based upon the Institutional Shareholders' Committee's (ISC) 'Code of Responsibilities of Institutional Investors'. However, the issue of investors' responsibilities, as countered by the dynamics of institutional investment, was on the agenda long before the Financial Crisis. Although not its main target, the 1992 Report from the Committee of the Financial Aspects of Corporate Governance, better known as the Cadbury Report because of the Chair of the Committee, Sir Adrian Cadbury, did focus on the important role that institutional investors have to play.

As Cheffins summarises, the Report devoted a chapter to encouraging increased dialogue between investors and the Boards of the companies they invest in. This proposed increase was to be systematically developed and was aligned to calls for investors to utilise the rights that came with their investment, like the ability to vote. However, the target for the Cadbury Committee was to install groundbreaking standards relating to the wider concept of corporate governance (which it did) and, as a result, the encouragement aimed at investors was left at that; '...it opted not to include any explicit references to shareholder engagement in its Code of Best Practice, which companies listed on the London Stock Exchange became obliged to adhere to on what was then a pioneering "comply-or-explain" basis (i.e. a listed company did not have to comply with provisions in the Code but had to disclose and explain instances of non-compliance in its annual report to shareholders)"'.[9]

The Committee on Corporate Governance's Report in 1998, better known as the Hampel Report after its Chair, Sir Ronald Hampel, was tasked with analysing the impact and development of the Cadbury Report.[10] It found that there was no need to revolutionise corporate governance in the UK but that were institutional investors were concerned, Cadbury's suggestions were good ones and that institutional shareholders should go further. In relation to pension fund trustees, the Hampel Committee urged them to put pressure on the fund managers they utilised to invest their assets in order to take a longer-term approach to executing their investment mandate.[11] The Hampel Report was acted upon with the transformation of the Cadbury Code of Best Practice into the 'Combined Code' and, in this new iteration, shareholders were directly addressed; Principles were articulated whereby direct guidance was given to both Boards and Shareholders to increase their communication.[12] This focus on the responsibility of the Board to consider the position of shareholders more was replicated and built upon in the Higgs Report in 2003.

There was clearly a push to respond to earlier failures (like the failures witnessed around the turn of the century with Enron, WorldCom, and others that brought auditors and Board constitutions into the regulatory light) but nothing would sharpen the regulatory mind more than the massive impact of the Financial Crisis upon the UK Banking scene. For the first time, at least relatively at the levels seen, the State would have to intervene and 'bail out' a number of high-profile banking entities. This high-profile assistance would be the spark that would ignite a new regulatory push, and the position of investors was very much on the political and regulatory agenda.

2.3 The Walker Review

The 'Walker Review', so-called after the Chair of the Review Sir David Walker, had a main focus on the UK Banking sector—as illustrated by the title of the Review ('A Review of Corporate Governance in UK Banks and other Financial Industry Entities: Final Recommendations).[13] Nevertheless, the Review was wide-ranging. In Chapter 5, Walker considers a number of key issues affecting the relationship between institutional investors and the companies they invest in. Ultimately, the Review adopts the position that shareholders need to take on the character of 'stewardship' if they are to contribute to the wider culture of effective corporate governance.[14] Furthermore, the already-promoted ideals of deeper communication between the two parties was additionally encouraged by Walker.[15] In the Review, Walker clearly articulates the recommended sentiment that the Review wants to put forward:

> As a matter of public interest, a situation in which the influence of major shareholders in their companies is principally executed through market transactions in the stock market cannot be regarded as a satisfactory ownership model, not least given the limited liability that shareholders enjoy.[16]

Walker was sharply focused on the industry's approach to signalling their dissatisfaction with the companies they invest in, and the ability to 'exit'[17] is highlighted early as being unsatisfactory (as above). Scholars were keen to pick up on Walker's identifying and, arguably, disdain for the fact that, 'according to Walker, "[they] enjoy the privilege of limited liability whereas taxpayers have ended up assuming unlimited liability in respect of the big banks. Early preventative medicine through shareholders engagement can save everyone substantial time and money later on"'.[18]

Walker continues this understanding in the fifth chapter of his Review:

> The potentially highly influential position of significant holders of stock in listed companies is a major ingredient in the market-based capitalist system

> which needs to earn and to be accorded an at least implicit social legitimacy. As counterpart to the obligation of the board to the shareholders, this implicit legitimacy can be acquired by at least the larger fund manager through assumption of a reciprocal obligation involving attentiveness to the performance of investee companies over a long as well as a short-term horizon. On this view, those who have significant rights of ownership and enjoy the very material advantage of limited liability should these as complemented by a duty of stewardship. This is a view that would be shared by the public, as well as those employees and suppliers who are less well-placed than an institutional shareholder to diversify their exposure to the management and performance risk of a limited liability company.[19]

Respondents to the consultation relating to the process were clear that they did not see their role as 'micro-managing' the companies they were invested in, which is a common response to the call for investors to play a larger role in the monitoring of their investee companies. It is for this reason that Walker declared that 'compliance with [the Code's] directives by shareholders "does not constitute an invitation to manage the affairs of investee companies"'.[20] Despite the guidance being put in place for pathways for more involvement from shareholders, the plan faced criticism on the basis of the negative effect of both the fragmentation of the investor markets, and the lack of applicability to foreign investors who may hold shares in the same companies that British-based investors also hold shares in.[21]

Nevertheless, Walker ultimately recommended that a separate 'Stewardship Code' should be established, based on the earlier ISC Principles (from the ISC Code of Responsibilities), and for it to be controlled by the Financial Reporting Council. The proposal was that the act of stewardship should be separated from the Corporate Governance Code and given its own place. It was also proposed that the Financial Services Authority (now the Financial Conduct Authority) 'should require institutions that are authorised to manage assets for others to disclose clearly on their websites or in other accessible form the nature of their commitment to the Stewardship Code'.[22] The FRC 'strongly encouraged' institutional investors to report if and how they complied with the new Code,[23] which Walker proposed be built upon the same comply-or-explain basis as the Corporate Governance Code. In reality, what Walker focused on was not developing a new Code bespoke for the investor sector, but the legitimising of an existing structure, namely the then newly developed ISC 'Code'.[24] In his 17th recommendation, Walker recommends that the ISC

Code 'should be ratified by the FRC and become the Stewardship Code. By virtue of the independence and authority of the FRC, this transition to sponsorship by the FRC should give materially greater weight to the Stewardship Code'.

With the FRC tasked with implementing these recommendations, the stage was set for the first formal Stewardship Code to be put in place. However, implementing a policy proposal is not the easiest task, and the FRC was about to embark upon a journey that, when combined with failures in the future relating to corporate collapses that dominated the headlines, would culminate in it being disbanded. So, how did the FRC implement Walker's recommendations?

2.4 The Dreaded Task of Implementation

The FRC accepted the task of implementing Walker's imagined Stewardship Code and in 2010 published its work.[25] The FRC had proudly declared that the Stewardship Code was 'the tool that would help improve the complex relationship between investors and investee companies'. However, the consultation was 'rushed' over a six-month period and, ultimately, the Code was published without making any significant change to the ISC Code that was the basis. As Reisberg states, 'in other words, a 20-year-old second-hand code was simply rebranded and sold to us as a new one'.[26] This was not, according to the Review's text, what Walker had in mind.

Jumping ahead slightly, the 2010 Code was revised in 2012. The additions were slight, consisting of mainly some guidance notes and some introductory text in places.[27] The reason we bring this up here is to demonstrate that the need for such revision is perhaps indicative of the rushed nature of the original 2010 Code. Sergekis, in his detailed exploration, describes how the 2010 Code did not provide much clarification on how investors would meet all of the responsibilities illustrated in the new Code. Additionally, whilst attempts were made in the initial Code to indicate who the Code applied to, there was a distinct lack of detail which 'left room for improvement'.[28] In a further demonstration of the lack of amendment to the ISC's Code, the FRC stated that there were Seven Principles of the Code which, remarkably, were exactly the same as the ISC's Seven Principles, namely:

So as to protect and enhance the value that accrues to the ultimate beneficiary, institutional investors should:

1. Publicly disclose their policy on how they will discharge their stewardship responsibilities;
2. Have a robust policy on managing conflicts of interest in relation to stewardship which should be publicly disclosed;
3. Monitor their investee companies;
4. Establish clear guidelines on when and how they will escalate their stewardship activities;
5. Be willing to act collectively with other investors where appropriate;
6. Have a clear policy on voting and disclosure of voting activity;
7. Report periodically on their stewardship and voting activities.[29]

Sergekis' article neatly picks apart each principle, but if we look at how the FRC chose to implement the Code and compare it to the underlying ISC Code upon which it is built, interesting patterns start to emerge. One example is the issue of managing conflicts of interest, which is naturally an important component of good governance. Sergekis notes that in the 2007 ISC Statement of Principles, it is made clear that institutional investors should not only declare any conflicts and how they may be managed, but crucially what actions are to be taken to *reduce* those conflicts. In the 2010/12 Stewardship Code, the requirement was merely to explain how such conflicts would be managed. The removal of responsibility to reduce conflicts of interests has been noted to be a compromise from the FRC even though 'there was "strong support for improved disclosure around conflicts of interest" from respondents to the consultation document during the recent revision of the Code [in 2012]'.[30] There is perhaps a reason for this that we will look at in much more detail in the last chapter of the book—just how does the FRC monitor such actions anyway, how do they enforce it, and do they have the authority to take punitive action for those who fail to meet the articulated standard? These are questions that plague the regulator. The issue of 'softness' is something that is consistently applied to the FRC and its impact.[31] For example, the 2012 amended Code has been accused of taking a 'soft approach' because, in reality, a large majority of the Code's targets *already adhered to the ISC Code*, which is why it has been said that the Code is merely a 'restatement of existing industry practices'.[32] Perhaps an argument could be put forward that this is what Walker called for in providing authority to the ISC Code by way of the FRC forcing it through, but many critics argue that the FRC was supposed to use the ISC Code as a *basis* and build a bespoke Code for the industry with larger-scale objectives in mind.

In summation, Roach suggests that the Code can be seen as operating of four levels. First, the FRC 'expects' fund managers to disclose their level of compliance with the Code. Second, the FRC 'strongly encourages' other institutional investors to report on how they comply with the code. Third, the FRC 'encourages' voting service agencies and other consultants to disclose how they carry out the wishes of their clients. Fourth, the FRC 'hopes' that overseas investors will commit to the Code and that the Code will become a beacon for stewardship. It is not difficult, therefore, to see why Roach follows this up with the understanding that 'the general consensus regarding the ISC Code is that it does not go far enough and does not impose high enough standards'.[33] If this was the belief of the ISC Code, then the understanding is that the Stewardship Code, which has been identified as being potentially weaker than the ISC Code, is not much better. It has been suggested that the issue with this understanding is that with the Stewardship Code 2010 and the amended 2012 version being the first of its kind, there is a likelihood that other jurisdictions will follow suit (which happened, in part) and that, as such, 'it is unfortunate that the world's first Stewardship Code was established on the basis of expeditiousness rather than a desire to establish a comprehensive and forward-looking set of engagement principles and must therefore be regarded as a missed opportunity to encourage greater investor engagement, not only in the UK but also around the world'.[34]

The post-Crisis era, with regards to investor stewardship, could therefore be seen as an attempt to start the ball rolling. Yet, it is more likely that the ball was fumbled because of a lack of concerted action and resourced endeavour. In the decade that followed, the concept of sustainable business practices across the financial sector would come to the fore and the role of investors—and in the modern world we really mean the role of institutional investors—would be brought to the fore like never before. As the concept of 'ESG' (Environment, Social, and Governance) was to become common parlance, an *effective* framework would be called for to harness the theoretical capability of investors to play a stronger part in the effective running of modern business. Next, we shall assess that build-up in order to understand how we have arrived at the most recent iteration of the Stewardship drive—the Stewardship Code 2020.

2.5 Conclusion

The call to place more emphasis on the role of institutional investors in the wake of the Financial Crisis was, in hindsight, a natural one. The lack of monitoring and enforcement from shareholders in the lead-up to the Crisis was a constituent part of the failure. Whilst traditional understandings of the ownership structures of corporate bodies have become particularly tested by the modern development of an institutional investor, the idea that shareholders have a role to play in governing the companies they are invested in has maintained, rightly or wrongly. One of the most important issues that lays beneath the surface of everything we are discussing here is that there is a fine balancing act with the issue of corporate responsibility. Institutional shareholders, just like the old theorised understanding of a 'shareholder', hold such shares for profit. With profit being the guiding factor, reducing costs is paramount. Institutional investors have quite rightly identified that it is more cost-efficient to 'exit' a shareholding rather than engaging with the company in question (as a generalisation). The act of diversification, which for a long time by economists and businesspeople has been championed as the correct approach to investing, is a direct cause of this problem. There have been suggestions that investors could have their ability to diversify 'capped' in order to focus their efforts on engagement rather than 'walking'.[35] This makes sense when viewed in isolation, but when viewed in context highlights one of the most important aspects that is not often overtly considered in the literature; all of this is operating within a *capitalist* system.

Capitalism is founded on the concept of accruing profit and utilising opportunities within the system to derive increases in capital. What some are proposing is a fundamental change to that economic and societal system. The chances of that happening are almost zero. If we look for a reason why the Stewardship Code is a Code, and not a law, then that is it. The State, via organs like the FRC (in its current form, although the FRC is not backed by Statute and started life in a very different manner), may very tentatively be trying to 'nudge' the system in a particular direction so as to avoid systemic collapses, but that is in reality all that they can do. An evolved capitalist system like that in the UK or the US is built upon the concept of an open market. In the next section where we look at the decade that followed the first Stewardship Code, the political backdrop must always be considered. Both the UK and the US electorate voted in 'conservative' governments that prioritised the predominant understandings of capitalism: open markets, less intrusive regulatory frameworks, and ultimately a pro-business narrative. Calls for 'hard law' to be utilised as a 'stick' against the 'carrot' of a 'soft law' approach that financial sectors get to mould and voluntarily assign themselves to can be seen as mis-directions at best because the political landscape post-Crisis is of crucial importance for our understanding; the answer to the collapsing of standards within high-finance has been to obtain the support of those in high-finance regarding the way forward. That understanding makes clear what is possible. The FRC, with its lack of statutory authority, has always been a sitting duck for political criticism when, in reality, that is arguably its role—to act as the lightning rod for criticism when, in fact, it is a systemic problem that the inefficiency of the FRC actually represents. We finish with this open-ended question: is there really an appetite by politicians, legislators, and regulators to do any more than what the FRC has done with the call for more to be done with regards to stewardship in the financial sector? In the next chapter, we will see how the different parties—regulators, politicians, and business—have responded to this issue.

Notes

1. Zhong Xing Tan, 'Stewardship in the Interests of Systemic Stakeholders: Re-conceptualising the Means and Ends of Anglo-American Corporate Governance in the Wake of the Global Financial Crisis' (2014) 9 *Journal of Business & Technology Law* 2 170, 169–212.
2. Arad Reisberg, 'The Notion of Stewardship from a Company Law Perspective' (2011) 18 *Journal of Financial Crime* 2 126, 126–47.
3. Peter Butler and Simon Wong, 'Recent Trends in Institutional Investor Responsibilities and Stewardship' (2011) 16 *Pensions* 82, 80–5 citing OECD, *Corporate Governance and the Financial Crisis: Key Findings and Main Messages* (2009) https://www.oecd.org/corporate/ca/corporategovernanceprinciples/43056196.pdf, 53.
4. Ibid.
5. Ibid.
6. Andrew Haldane, *Patience and Finance* (2010) https://www.bis.org/review/r100909e.pdf, 10.
7. Justin Fox and Jaw W Lorsch, 'What Good Are Shareholders?' (2012) *Harvard Business Review* (July–August) https://hbr.org/2012/07/what-good-are-shareholders.

8. Konstantinos Sergekis, 'The UK Stewardship Code: Bridging the Gap Between Companies and Institutional Investors' (2013) 47 *Revue Juridique Themis* 1 117, 109–154.
9. Brian R Cheffins, 'The Stewardship Code's Achilles' Heel' (2010) 73 *Modern Law Review* 6 1007, 1004–5.
10. Committee on Corporate Governance, *Final Report* (1998) https://ecgi.global/sites/default/files/codes/documents/hampel.pdf.
11. Cheffins (n 9) 1008.
12. Ibid.
13. The Walker Review, *A Review of Corporate Governance in UK Banks and Other Financial Industry Entities: Final Recommendations* (2009) https://webarchive.nationalarchives.gov.uk/+/http:/www.hm-treasury.gov.uk/d/walker_review_261109.pdf.
14. Mads Andenas and Iris H-Y Chiu, *The Foundations and Future of Financial Regulation: Governance for Responsibility* (Routledge 2013) 393.
15. Roger Barker, 'The New Governance of UK Finance: Implementing the Walker Review' (2010) 25 International Banking and Financial Law 5 298.
16. The Walker Review (n 13) 70.
17. Sergekis (n 8) 143.
18. Tihir Sarkar, Simon Jay, and Garry Manley, 'An Analysis of the Walker Review of Corporate Governance in U.K. Banks and Other Financial Institutions' (2010) 127 *Banking Law Journal* 3 242, 242–51.
19. The Walker Review (n 13) 70.
20. Jennifer G Hill, 'Regulating Executive Remuneration After the Global Financial Crisis: Common Law Perspectives' in Randall S. Thomas and Jennifer G. Hill, *Research Handbook on Executive Pay* (Edward Elgar 2012) 229.
21. Ibid.
22. Sarkar et al. (n 18) 246.
23. Lorraine Talbot, *Progressive Corporate Governance for the 21st Century* (Routledge 2013) 182.
24. Jacqui Hatfield and Gil Cohen, 'The UK Walker Review: What Banks Should Do Now' (2009) 28 *International Financial Law Review* 9.
25. Jill Solomon, *Corporate Governance and Accountability* (John Wiley & Sons 2020) 52.
26. Arad Reisberg, 'The UK Stewardship Code: On the Road to Nowhere?' (2015) 15 *Journal of Corporate Law Studies* 2 222, 217–53.
27. Sergekis (n 8) 122.
28. Ibid 124.
29. Financial Reporting Council, *The UK Stewardship Code* (2012) https://www.frc.org.uk/getattachment/d67933f9-ca38-4233-b603-3d24b2f62c5f/UK-Stewardship-Code-(September-2012).pdf, 5.

30. Sergekis (n 8) 127.
31. Tabby Kinder, 'UK Watchdog Triples Fines on Accountancy Firms' (2019) *Financial Times* (July 31) https://www.ft.com/content/594c8bf2-b2e8-11e9-8cb2-799a3a8cf37b.
32. Sergekis (n 8) 132.
33. Lee Roach, 'The UK Stewardship Code' (2011) 11 *Journal of Corporate Law Studies* 2 464, 463–93.
34. Ibid 478.
35. Sergekis (n 8) 143.

CHAPTER 3

A Decade of Development

3.1 Introduction

It is unsurprising that, with the establishment of the first Stewardship Code to be backed by a regulator, there was to be plenty of analysis and potentially criticism that followed. The need for impact was clear, and if one marries to this the hope that was present before the establishment of the Code, the level of interest is understandable. We know now in hindsight, given there was a quick revision to the Code, and that there is now a new Code, that the Stewardship Code 2010 and 2012 were very much early milestones in the development of formalised Stewardship Codes. In the years that followed, the focus was very much on how to develop the Code to better suit the business environment.

Yet, the criticism of the way the Code was established, the approach taken by the regulator, and the regulator itself were all significant. Key deficiencies were to be highlighted with the end of the decade proving to be massively impactful for the future of the FRC. We should keep the systemic issues discussed at the end of the last chapter in mind at all times, but a number of technical aspects were assessed after the establishment of the 2010 Code. We will reiterate some of the aspects of the last chapter here as, on occasion, the elements that were revealed in the immediate aftermath of the establishment of the 2010 Code continued to be of great interest and impacted upon developments towards the new Code. This chapter will focus on these technical aspects before returning to our story

D. Cash and R. Goddard, *Investor Stewardship and the UK Stewardship Code*, https://doi.org/10.1007/978-3-030-87152-9_3

of the development of the new 2020 Code. Such technical analysis is vitally important because they allow us to gauge both the reasoning for the changes in 2020, the reasoning for what was to happen to the FRC, and also (crucially) the chances of success for the new 2020 Code.

3.2 Main Criticisms of the First Codes

The original 2010 Stewardship Code and, by extension the 2012 version, faced some strong criticism concerning two distinctive but interrelated aspects:

- Questions about the wider system in which stewardship takes place. Additionally, challenges that affect the whole investment chain, including the issue of fiduciary duties and the alignment of interests between asset owners and managers.
- The challenges related to stewardship regulation and its implementation by asset managers in the UK. Examples include the definition of stewardship within the Stewardship Code, and the ownership and constitution of companies listed in the United Kingdom.

Perhaps one of the main issues that underlay the effectiveness of the early Codes was the target of the Codes themselves. The target, in effect the investment chain itself, is arguably too long and, as a result, problematic.[1] For a person's pension contribution to be invested, there are many steps to be taken, for example. This length has the effect of, arguably, altering the mindset[2] of those who ultimately invest the fund, as the disassociation from the principal investor can lead to a weakening of accountability and responsibility structures that really need to be present when investing the resources of others.[3] This disconnect is the fundamental problem with the wider system in which stewardship takes place.

If we maintain focus on the length of the investment chain, then it stands to reason that there will be a number of 'pinch-points' in the chain where costs are incurred, as more and more experts and professional find a place that is created to assist with the functioning of the chain. This is often done under the guise of cost efficiency. However, it may not be so efficient, as the increase in the number of people/organisations has the potential to lead to increase in conflicts of interests, as each seeks to generate fees for their services. This can affect, crucially, decision-making processes along the chain.[4] All of these factors are likely to impact upon the returns of the ultimate beneficiary of investments. The crux of the problem with the investment chain was summarised in a 2008 study about pension plans: 'There is a widespread perception in the pension world that the investment industry is perverse in one crucial sense: its food chain operates in reverse, with service providers at the top and clients at the bottom. Agents fare better than principals'.[5]

In order to counter these identified issues within the investment chain, the Kay Review endeavoured to recommend that the restraining concept of one having fiduciary duties be implemented along the chain, inclusive of all associated relationships.[6] In addition to calling for the imposition of duties to be applied to all parties, the Review simply recommended that the chain itself be radically shortened.[7] There is some evidence that this is happening in practice.[8]

The role of the major components of the investment chain has been analysed in the literature.[9] Barker and Chiu suggest that when one is invested in a company, there comes with that investment 'moral rights and obligations'.[10] One of the key suggestions is that there is a 'social interest' involved with investments and that, as such, there should be mechanisms in place that reflect that social interest-angle; for example, investors should have a long-term interest in their investment and should be willing to take a more active role in the governance of the company they are invested in.[11] This, of course, makes sense in theory. However, in reality, most asset owners are subject to particularly short-term pressures. These short-term pressures effectively govern the approach that an institutional investor can possibly take.[12] The scholars, interestingly, are left with nowhere to go other than to conclude that institutional investors do not have the capacity nor willingness to fully embrace the concept of effective stewardship.[13] There is scope to question the conclusion that there is not the willingness to embrace the concept, because a number of the factors that promote short-termism are external to the institutional investor, but the issue of *capacity* is likely more accurate.

Immediately after the publication of the early Codes, five underlying structural deficiencies within the investment industry were detailed: a 'misguided interpretation of fiduciary duty', 'inappropriate performance metrics and financial arrangements', 'excessive portfolio diversification' of asset managers, and problems within passive asset managers.[14] These identified deficiencies provide a useful structure for us to understand the issues that ultimately affected the success of the early Codes.

3.2.1 *The Issue of Fiduciary Duty*

The concept of one having a fiduciary duty is well established. The concept traditionally revolves around the requirement of one, who is in a position of control over another's interest, to act in the best interests of that other. That interest is related to the protection of another's *financial* interest, so that they may not, stereotypically, suffer an adverse financial consequence unnecessarily.[15] The issue with this traditional concept in the modern arena is that those aspects usually termed as being 'nonfinancial' in nature—factors generally categorised as Environmentally, Socially, or Governance-related, for example (ESG)—tend to be viewed as being in conflict with traditionally financial in nature factors. This serves to limit the scope of what an actor who is bound by fiduciary-related rules is usually willing to do.[16]

There have been attempts by scholars and professional bodies to make the connection between nonfinancial factors and the concept of being held responsible under fiduciary-related rules. One good example of this is the Law Commission's report in 2014,[17] as well as the work conducted by Freshfields Bruckhaus Deringer in 2005 on behalf of the UN Environment Programme (UNEP) Finance Initiative.[18] Yet, despite the theoretical advancements regarding the importance of considering nonfinancial elements, Tilba and Reisberg,[19] found with regard to pension funds and the responsibilities of their trustees, not much has changed in practice. Simply put, the scholars concluded that 'the relationship between fiduciary duties and stewardship is ambiguous' and that there is a 'fuzziness' of the applicable duties in the context of pension funds.[20] The result of this is that anything that can be outside of the 'core purpose' of an institutional investor i.e. focusing on financial returns, is considered to be outside of the scope of what one's fiduciary duty may be.[21]

It is understood that something will need to change when it comes to the applicability of the concept of fiduciary duties when related to nonfinancial information. Whilst there has been a number of pronouncements from a variety of bodies and sectors, like multilateral institutions such as the UN[22] or from private market participants like Ernst & Young,[23] the reality is that the issue of the applicability of nonfinancial considerations to the concept of fiduciary duties is extremely messy.[24] It strongly appears that traditional parameters associated with one's fiduciary duties are proving hard to move past.[25] It is perhaps not too difficult to empathise with asset owners and managers who fear the liability that comes with breaching one's fiduciary duties, given the reverence those duties have been (rightly) prescribed since company law emerged across modern markets. This is not to defend such hesitance, but throw-away comments in reports have little bearing on the underlying fact that it is the law that must change, or at least make clear that nonfinancial considerations will not result in a breach of one's duties, before the issue can be truly resolved.

3.2.2 *Asset Owners and Managers: The Need for Alignment*

Asset owners often employ asset managers to invest their resources for them, for a fee. One of the main reasons for this is that it is often more cost effective to do so. Asset managers can focus on the business of investing, deploy their resources to ensure, as much as possible, that the resources are invested in the best possible areas to generate returns. What binds the two together is something called an *investment mandate*, which is essentially a contractually binding set of rules that the asset owner will prescribe and which the manager must comply with. This can range from a number of approaches, and may involve screening or particular selections of industries within which one can invest (for example, one may constrain a manager so that they do not invest in fossil-fuel-related businesses).

Therefore, alignment between the two parties is crucial. Investment mandates, arguably, therefore stand as one of the most promising vehicles within which more responsible investing practices can be encouraged across the investment sphere. They can spell out agreements on aspects such as fees to be paid, and when. However, they can also include aspects of stewardship and responsible practice to be undertaken when deploying the asset owner's resources. There still exists the issue of answering to one's principals, which potentially blunts the true potential of the investment mandate to bring about better investment practices, but they are technically the vehicle for dictating better investment practices.

The aspects that can blunt to the potential of investment mandates to create a change in investment culture are many. If there are misalignments (and there often are) between the two parties relating to aspects such as size, complexity within the organisation, maturity, and necessary time horizons, then the result can be ineffectiveness built into the mandate itself. When it comes to stewardship behaviour and responsible practice, these are often casualties of the misalignment. There is usually a standard mandate that is used as a foundation, upon which the two parties essentially indicate the factors that affect their respective positions.[26] For example, a smaller asset owner will likely be in a worse bargaining position when contracting with a larger asset manager (and vice versa).[27]

As with regards to the injection of stewardship concerns into the investment mandate, there is clearly the need to align interests of both the parties to a longer time horizon.[28] There have been attempts to create a model set of contractual terms that can allow this objective to be met.[29] There are a number of factors that could be added to investment mandates which have been suggested would aid with achieving this goal, ranging from the inclusion of ESG to remuneration standards.[30] However, there are some key issues which must be addressed in order to bring the time horizon considerations of both the parties closer together. First, the ability of the asset owner to cancel the contract at will leads to a short-termist approach from the manager, for fear of having their services rendered obsolete.[31] Second, asset owners often have to signal to their beneficiaries the state of affairs. To do this, the traditional approach is to report quarterly to one's beneficiary base. To do this then, an asset owner's managers must be able to demonstrate progress on a quarterly basis. This, clearly, is not conducive to a long-term approach.[32] With regards to stewardship, this disincentivises a manager (or owner) to engage with an investee company on matters that will crystallise in the medium- to long-term.[33] Lastly (although one could argue there are many more issues), the fee structures for managers are potentially skewed towards promoting short-termism. Fees are often calculated on a fixed percentage for assets-under-management (AUM), with discounts based on the amounts to be managed.[34] This results in the incentive being with regard to the assets gathered rather than the assets managed.[35]

3.2.3 *The Realities of the Implementation of a Stewardship Code*

The Stewardship Code 2010, and the amendments in the 2012 version, contained a number of key issues which came to define its chances of success. With the Code being the first to be formally enacted by a regulator, communication over what the Code was, aimed to do, who it impacted, and what Stewardship even meant, was all key. However, to the dismay of many, little of those necessary communications were forthcoming. Reisberg discusses the fact that there was not even a definition of what stewardship is in the very first Stewardship Code! Clearly then the confusion and divergence that followed could almost be described as a natural reaction.[36] Furthermore, what was expected from the Code of the various players within the investment chain was itself not made clear.[37] Even the addition of an introductory section in the 2012 version fell short according to scholars, as the suggestion was that it only aimed to explain what stewardship aims to achieve, rather than the responsibilities of the parties involved.[38]

What is also interesting is that the Stewardship Codes operate on a comply-or-explain basis, but with little definitional foundation which was obviously a cause for concern. As scholars noted, this is also problematic because the oversight of an entity's compliance usually sat with the asset owner, not the FRC who took a passive role to oversight and enforcement.[39] The lack of a statutory underpinning, or even support from industry norms like the Listing Rules, meant that the Codes had hardly any teeth whatsoever. The FRC monitored disclosure compliance, rather than the actual implementation and practice of stewardship principles; this was identified as being a key issue by scholars and those tasked with reviewing the state of affairs, as we shall see shortly.

3.3 The Kingman Review

The Kingman Review can be seen as the accumulation of anti-FRC sentiment in the UK. After two Select Committees found the regulator to be failing on a number of fronts, the Review essentially formalised this sentiment and set the regulator forward on a path it could not recover from. The Select Committees had found evidence of failure to change regulatory approaches when appropriate, shortcomings in the way it monitored the regulated, and ultimately a lack of authority—particularly ranging from the fact that the FRC had no real legal foundation like other regulators have.[40] The FRC had been labelled as 'toothless', 'timid', 'chronically passive', and 'useless' and, as such, the Secretary of State requested that Kingman undertake the Review.[41] It is noted that the initial aim was to explore ways of improving the FRC, but with the findings of the Review being so critical the question of improving the FRC was upgraded to whether there instead needed to be an entirely new regulator.[42]

The focus on the FRC made for difficult reading for the regulator. In searching for root causes to the identified failures, Kingman focuses on the reality that, unlike its fellow regulators, the FRC is not really a regulator in the traditional and particularly legal senses. He makes the following points as to why the FRC is different to other regulators:

- It did not start out as a regulator
- It had no meaningful statutory base, unlike other regulators
- It did not start out as a public body, but a private one
- Its Board is largely self-perpetuating, with Government intervention only being seen regarding the Chair and Deputy Chair
- The 'Council' element of the FRC's name is representative of its non-regulatory nature.[43]

Whilst the tone of the Review was negative for the FRC, Kingman does make clear that he both understands the reasoning for ineffectiveness, but also the good work that the FRC have done, with particular reference to maintaining the Corporate Governance Code and its development.[44] Nevertheless, for Kingman the devolved structure of the regulator was a major issue. He notes that in a number of different areas, the 'FRC's powers are limited or even non-existent, leaving it in the unfortunate situation of having been given responsibility without power'.[45]

However, the FRC's practice was also heavily called into question. Kingman concluded that the FRC's relationships with the investment community were lacking. Whilst not putting all of the blame on the FRC for this lack of relationship, aspects such as the late development of a forum for investors and the regulator were cited as key examples of a lack of action. He adds to this the lack of transparency that has engulfed the regulator, as evidenced by the fact that Freedom of Information provisions do not apply to all of the FRC's statutory functions, with a lack of transparency being identified in other key areas of the FRC's mandate.[46] These aspects, amongst others (particularly the lack of a legal foundation) led the Review to conclude that 'the FRC does not command the same credibility as that of the Public Companies Accounting Oversight Board (PCAOB) in the USA in the area of audit quality'.[47]

As part of the consultation phase for the Review, a number of questions were asked of the field. The ICAEW (Institute of Chartered Accountants in England and Wales), who are understandably a major player in the UK, were unequivocal in their criticism of the FRC (in particular areas). Issues of a lack of communication with the regulated, a lack of foresight on potential impact from regulatory endeavours, and a poor approach to penalising were all cited. Also, the ICAEW noted that the FRC was overly-focused on compliance, which it believes has led to an inflexibility that has plagued the regulator. This is, according to the ICAEW, paired with an over-defensiveness when challenged, which all leads to a rigid regulator in a field were a dynamic approach is perhaps required. Interestingly, the ICAEW challenges the notion that the FRC is 'feeble' and 'timid', instead discussing their interaction with a forceful and sometimes excessively-demanding regulator. Like Kingman, the ICAEW do acknowledge some of the good work the FRC has done, whilst also making the revealing claim that with the lack of statutory authority behind it, the FRC can be considered to be a 'scapegoat' in certain circumstances; as the ICAEW state, 'the FRC cannot do what it is not empowered to do'.[48]

Irrespective of the green shoots of successful regulating, the mountain of evidence indicating structural deficiencies appears to have been too great. As part of the Review, Kingman proposed the development of an entirely new regulator, to be called the Audit, Reporting and Governance Authority (ARGA). In March 2019, the UK announced that it would heed this recommendation and that the FRC would be disbanded as a result.[49] It is expected that ARGA will be in place and everything ready for the transition in 2023. Kingman discusses how the new regulator should be developed to be an 'improvement regulator', with the example of how the Civil Aviation Authority engages with the Airline industry being cited as a good example to follow—although Kingman does acknowledge the very different financial incentives that affect members of the Airline industry as opposed to members of the audit industry, for example. Interestingly, he makes clear that the new regulator cannot be a 'soft regulator' and that 'what it should do is use all the available levers it has—including robust enforcement and the powerful deterrent effect this can create—to maximise self-reinforcing incentives to pursue quality and best practice'.[50] Other declarations by Kingman are more difficult to predict how they will be executed, and whilst we will look at this more in the final chapter, Kingman's call for the new regulator to 'take responsibility for improvement over and above checking the work of others' is not so straightforward. This is of particular interest when we think of the concept of the Stewardship Code and what it aims to contribute to the financial sector (and further afield).

The 2012 Code came under scrutiny in the Review as well, and the findings were equally as damning. Perhaps the most important aspect for Kingman was that the Code had no basis in law, and whilst Asset Managers were required by the FCA's Conduct of Business Rules to disclose whether or not they were complying, the lack of legal basis left the Code to become a very soft-touch mechanism. In joining the calls for a new and improved Stewardship Code (which would become the Stewardship Code 2020 which we turn to in the next chapter), Kingman highlights one of the key deficiencies in that the current regulatory approach is to recognise the statements made by the regulated, rather than the actual effectiveness or outcome generated by those statements. He sees this as a major factor, ultimately declaring that:

> The Review recommends that a fundamental shift in approach is needed to ensure that the revised Stewardship Code more clearly differentiates excellence in stewardship. It should focus on outcomes and effectiveness, not on policy statements. The Government should also consider whether any further powers are needed to assess and promote compliance with the Code. If the Code remains simply a driver of boilerplate reporting, serious considerations should be given to its abolition.[51]

He continues by declaring that the old Code 'is not effective in practice'.[52] It is therefore not surprising that commentators have suggested that the new Code is the 'last throw of the dice'.[53] Others have agreed that if the new Code does not make a bigger impact, then the concept of having a Stewardship Code should be scrapped entirely.[54] It is questionable whether this is the case, mostly because of the ever-growing importance of the concept of responsible business practices to which investors have been (correctly) intrinsically aligned to.

The Review was widely accepted, and its recommendations supported. Yet, there are issues worth highlighting. Walker-Arnott is very critical of the Review, stating that 'a fast review leading to a quick conclusion on the central issue has meant that the report contains errors and inconsistencies which detract from its authority and important considerations are inadequately researched and analysed'.[55] Of particular note are the 'inadequacies of the Review's analysis of the serious and wider issues of directors' responsibilities for true and fair accounting, and of the nature and content of interaction between directors and auditors in the course of the preparation and audit of annual accounts'.[56] This can be seen also in the lack of analysis of just how the regulator will seek to truly monitor the actions (or inaction) of the regulated in relation to the Stewardship

Code. Davies also notes that whilst it is widely but anecdotally accepted that shareholder engagement has not significantly improved as a result of the original Codes, Kingman undertook no empirical research whatsoever, which is problematic when proposing an entirely new regulator partly on the basis of said ineffectiveness.[57] He also makes the very valid argument that the dynamic underlying all of these issues—the fine balance between allowing for autonomy in the marketplace but providing for a focused and directed structure—is far beyond the capability of the FRC and whatever Review is analysing the issues, but that this has not stopped people opining on what needs to happen. Ultimately, Davies shares the sentiment that theory and practice are still too far apart and that some of the recommendations only serve to perpetuate this issue.

3.3.1 International Impact

Despite issues with the 2012 Code, it was influential on the global scene. Japan followed shortly after with its 2014 Code, with a number of countries following on and increasing the momentum in the stewardship world.[58] Interestingly, the influence of the Code spread far beyond the West, with a large number of Asian jurisdictions also adopting their own versions of a Stewardship Code.[59] In the EU, the decision was taken to amend the Shareholder Rights Directive in 2017, creating what is widely known as the Shareholder Rights Directive II (SRD II).[60] Whilst the first SRD was focused on developing base Company Law issues in the bloc, the amendment focused on addressing the role that shareholders play within corporations, and it has been said that the Articles in the Directive 'appear to be derived from the [2012] UK Stewardship Code'.[61]

The similarities between the UK Stewardship Code and the SRD II proclamations are perhaps clear. The SRD II also focuses on shareholder engagement and applies a comply-or-explain model,[62] whilst it also obliges its targets to disclose how it approaches its stewardship activities.[63] However, there is an important point to understand before we continue and the differences between the UK Stewardship Code and the SRD II provide us with a perfect example; the principles and objectives underlying the concept of stewardship, and particularly how a jurisdiction views those principles and objectives, is certainly not universal. There are a number of traditional and cultural values that will affect how a Stewardship Code or approach is designed and implemented. For example, Chiu argues that whilst the UK Stewardship Code and the SRD II rules look similar, they are actually very different.

Apart from having a 'different tenor from the empowering language in the Code', Chiu argues that the biggest difference is that the SRD II applies to *all* institutional investors, rather than being on a voluntary and signatory approach.[64] Another major difference, according to Chiu, is that the EU takes a normative approach to the task, essentially declaring through its rulings that engagement should be considered as inherent within the role of a shareholder.[65] Chiu contrasts the whole approach with that of the UK, arguing that the cultural factors affecting the development of rules comes to fruition in how the regulators view the role of shareholders. She argues that, in the UK, shareholders are regarded as 'enlightened', and that the whole process is regarded as being 'private' in nature. This issue of the arena being a private one means that there is a reluctance to interfere, which is why the issues that arise from the concept of one having a fiduciary duty to one's beneficiaries—which should not be externally altered to any great extent by regulation—are so prevalent in the UK. Chiu contrasts this approach with that of the EU, where it is argued that the whole concept of corporate governance and also stewardship (if we consider this to be separate) is publicised (or at least that is the aim).[66]

Other works provide the necessary detail on the SRD II[67] and it is, unfortunately, beyond our remit here. However, the key point for us is that there are different understandings of the same concept. Politics, but also national identity, tradition, and culture all play a part of impacting the design, development, implementation, and continuation of a Stewardship Code. This point is so important to remember as we move into the next chapter, which looks at the all-new Stewardship Code that has been brought into practice in the UK. Rather than reflexively reacting to a Crisis, the new Code has been purposively designed and it takes into account a number of forces that are impacting corporate governance and stewardship thinking. The question is whether the new direction is achievable, and what part it plays in the trajectory of stewardship in the UK. If the original Code was influential on the global scene, it stands to reason that the stewardship world will be watching the developments in the UK closely.

3.4 Conclusion

The first-ever formalised Stewardship Codes were a welcome development in the wake of the Financial Crisis. In line with other movements in the financial arena, like that of responsible and sustainable investment practices or the emergence of the consideration of ESG, promoting better practices and injecting the concept of stewardship into the institutional investor's realm was surely positive. The aim to promote ideals of more engagement where appropriate, better communication, and more accountability are to be lauded.

However, the gap between theory and practice are far too often overlooked. Pushing for change when the potential impacts have not been fully considered can cause more harm than good. The rushed development of the original Code, the early revision, and the progression into major Reviews that called for the disintegration of the regulator have left a sour taste. Now, the new Stewardship Code has an incredible amount of pressure placed upon it when in fact it is important to see such endeavours as evolutionary. In keeping with modern sentiment, it has instead been labelled as 'do-or-die', succeed or fail. This sentiment is unhelpful.

The calls by the Kingman Review for the new Code to be latterly maintained and grown by a new regulator is also potentially harmful. We do not know how the new regulator will start, develop, and impact the field. The old Codes were perhaps based upon a very soft approach that regulators in this field cannot harden; is there really an appetite to take a harder approach to regulating in the field of stewardship? Should investors be left to decide, for the most part, when they intervene and engage and when they do not? Is there really an appetite to prescribe when a private investor should engage with the company they are invested in, irrespective of whether it is a 'public' company or not. There are fundamental issues that underlie developments in this crucial sector of private investment, and it is questionable how much this was considered in the post-Crisis era.

Nevertheless, action was taken. A new regulator was proposed, and plans are in place for that regulator to carry the torch. A new Stewardship Code was requested and the FRC have now developed the Stewardship Code 2020 and are currently in the process of receiving the first round of reports. What is clear is that the pressure within the system, more than a decade on from the first actions taken to resolve issues brought to the fore in the Financial Crisis, is mounting. It is perhaps remarkable that a 'solution' is now fundamentally required just ten years on from the first-ever Stewardship Code, but that is perhaps the reality of the modern thought process. In the next chapter, we assess the new Code and move into the final stages of the book where we look more at how this underlying dynamic may affect actions to encourage more care and attention from investors.

Notes

1. The Kay Review of UK Equity Markets and Long-Term Decision Making (2012) https://assets.publishing.service.gov.uk/government/uploads/system/uploads/attachment_data/file/253454/bis-12-917-kay-review-of-equity-markets-final-report.pdf, 3.7–3.11.
2. Simon CY Wong, 'Why Stewardship is Proving to be Elusive for Institutional Investors' (2010) 7 *Journal of International Banking and Financial Law* 406.
3. Ibid 407.
4. Kay Review (n 1) 3.10.
5. Amin Rajan, *DB & DC Plans: Strengthening Their Delivery* (Create 2008) 10.
6. Kay Review (n 1) Recommendation 7 (Chapter 9). Lee called this recommendation one of the two most important ones of the Kay Review, see Lee (2012), 7.
7. Kay Review (n 1), 6.13.
8. Simon CY Wong, 'Is Institutional Investor Stewardship Still Elusive?' (2015) 8 *Journal of International Banking and Financial Law* 508, 511.
9. Roger M Barker and Iris HY Chiu, *Corporate Governance and Investment Management: The Promises and Limitations of the New Financial Economy* (Edward Elgar 2017).
10. Ibid 437.
11. Ibid 438.
12. Ibid.
13. Ibid 440.
14. Wong (n 2) 406.
15. *Cowan v Scargill* [1985] 1 Ch. 270 Ch D.
16. Wong (n 2), 408–9.
17. Law Commission (2014), Fiduciary Duties of Investment Intermediaries (review concluded that there was no need to clarify the law). This was triggered by the Kay Review (n 1) which highlighted the need to clarify fiduciary duties and recommended a review by the Law Commission. Work by the Department of Work and Pensions in 2018 led to significant amendments of Occupational Pension Schemes (Investment) Regulations

2005 requiring the SIP to contain statements on ESG investments, non-financial considerations and stewardship policies.

18. Freshfields Bruckhaus Deringer, *A Legal Framework for the Integration of Environmental, Social and Governance Issues into Institutional Investment* (2005) https://www.unepfi.org/fileadmin/documents/freshfields_legal_resp_20051123.pdf.
19. Anna Tilba and Arad Reisberg, 'Fiduciary Duty under the Microscope: Stewardship and the Spectrum of Pension Fund Engagement' (2019) 82 *Modern Law Review* 3 456–87.
20. Ibid 486.
21. Ibid.
22. UNEP, *Fiduciary Duty in the 21st Century* (2019) https://www.unepfi.org/wordpress/wp-content/uploads/2019/10/Fiduciary-duty-21st-century-final-report.pdf.
23. EY, *ESG Investing under Fiduciary Management: Minds Made for Transforming Financial Services* (2018) https://assets.ey.com/content/dam/ey-sites/ey-com/en_gl/topics/emeia-financial-services/ey-esg-investing-under-fiduciary-management.pdf.
24. John Hill, *Environmental, Social, and Governance Investing: A Balanced Review of Theoretical Backgrounds and Practical Implications* (Elsevier 2020) 45–58.
25. Christopher K Merker and Sarah W Peck, *The Trustee Governance Guide: The Five Imperatives of 21st Century Investing* (Springer 2019) 15.
26. For example, The Investment Association, *A Model Discretionary Investment Management Agreement* (2018) https://www.theia.org/sites/default/files/2019-08/Model_IMA_website_version.pdf.
27. FCA, *Asset Management Market Study Final Report* (2017) 5.
28. FCLT, *Institutional Investment Mandates: Anchors for Long-term Performance* (2020) https://www.fcltglobal.org/wp-content/uploads/Institutional-Investment-Mandates-Anchors-for-Long-term-Performance_FCLTGlobal.pdf, 5.
29. ICGN, *Model Mandate* (2012) http://icgn.flpbks.com/icgn_model-contract-terms_2015.
30. ICGN *Consultation* (2020) summarising key aspects of the ICGN Model Mandate (2012) https://www.icgn.org/sites/default/files/GGP%20consultation%20June%202020.pdf.
31. FCLT (n 28) 7–8.
32. Ibid 8.
33. Wong (n 2) 406–7, and Wong (n 8) 509–10.
34. FCLT (n 28) 7.
35. Wong (n 2) 407.
36. Arad Reisberg, 'The UK Stewardship Code: On the Road to Nowhere?' (2015) 15 *Journal of Corporate Law Studies* 2 228, 217–53. The same

author highlighted this omission in a separate article in 2011, see Arad Reisberg, 'The Notion of Stewardship from a Company Law Perspective: Re-defined and Re-assessed in Light of the Recent Financial Crisis? (2011) 18 *Journal of Financial Crime* 2 133.

37. Arad Reisberg, 'The UK Stewardship Code: On the Road to Nowhere?' (2015) 15 *Journal of Corporate Law Studies* 2 228, 217–53.
38. Ibid 229.
39. Reisberg (n 37) 240–1.
40. Robert Baldwin and Martin Cave, *Taming the Corporation: How to Regulate for Success* (Oxford University Press 2020) 191.
41. Patrick Hosking, '"Toothless" Accountancy Watchdog Faces Inquiry' (2018) *The Times* (March 22) https://www.thetimes.co.uk/article/toothless-accountancy-watchdog-faces-inquiry-pmkxk73dv.
42. Jill Solomon, *Corporate Governance and Accountability* (John Wiley & Sons 2020) 54.
43. John Kingman, *Independent Review of the Financial Reporting Council* (2018) https://assets.publishing.service.gov.uk/government/uploads/system/uploads/attachment_data/file/767387/frc-independent-review-final-report.pdf, 6.
44. Charlotte Villiers and Georgina Tsagas, 'Accounting for Climate Change: Rethinking the Chaotic Corporate Reporting Landscape and its Purpose, with the UK's failure as a Case Study' in Margherita Pieraccini and Tonia Novitz. *Legal Perspectives on Sustainability* (Policy Press 2020) 83.
45. Kingman (n 43) 7.
46. Ibid 12.
47. Solomon (n 42).
48. ICAEW, *Review of the Financial Reporting Council by Sir John Kingman: ICAEW Submission* (2018) https://www.icaew.com/-/media/corporate/files/technical/icaew-representations/2018/icaew-rep-92-18-review-of-the-financial-reporting-council-by-sir-john-kingman.ashx, 9.
49. Baldwin and Cave (n 40).
50. Kingman (n 43) 22.
51. Ibid 46.
52. Ibid 12.
53. Martin Webster, 'FRC Responds to Kingman Criticism with Revised UK Stewardship Code' (2019) Pinsent Masons (January 31) https://www.pinsentmasons.com/out-law/news/frc-responds-to-kingman-criticism-with-revised-uk-stewardship-code.
54. Owen Walker, 'Beacon of British Stewardship Needs a Brighter Flame' (2019) *Financial Times* (January 27) https://www.ft.com/content/1a3a57be-5c15-3e03-bae0-10bd5804bf20.
55. Edward Walker-Arnott, 'The Kingman Review' (2019) 40 *Company Lawyer* 6 179, 179–85.

56. Ibid 184.
57. Paul L Davies, 'The UK Stewardship Code 2010–2010: From Saving the Company to Saving the Planet?' (2020) ECGI Working Paper Series 506/2020 9.
58. Kim M Willey, *Stock Market Short-Termism: Law, Regulation, and Reform* (Springer 2019) 99. Writing in 2019, Willey states that as of 31 March 2018, there were a total of 19 jurisdictions that had adopted some version of a stewardship code. See also Jennifer G Hill, 'Good Activist/Bad Activist: The Rise of International Stewardship Codes' (2018) 41 *Seattle University Law Review* 2 497–524.
59. Ernest Lim, *A Case for Shareholders' Fiduciary Duties in Common Law Asia* (Cambridge University Press 2019) 21. Lim cites Hong Kong, Malaysia, Singapore, and India as examples.
60. Directive 2017/828/EU.
61. Iris HY Chiu, 'European Shareholder Rights Directive proposals: A Critical Analysis in Mapping with the UK Stewardship Code?' (2016) 17 *ERA Forum* 31–44.
62. Hanne S Birkmose and Konstantinos Sergekis, *Enforcing Shareholders' Duties* (Edward Elgar 2019) 125.
63. Willey (n 58).
64. Chiu (n 61) 33.
65. Ibid 35.
66. Ibid 40.
67. Hanne S Birkmose and Konstantinos Sergekis, *The Shareholder Rights Directive II: A Commentary* (Edward Elgar 2021).

CHAPTER 4

The Stewardship Code 2020

4.1 Introduction

The lead-up to the publication of the Stewardship Code 2020 was not an easy one for the FRC. Responses to consultations were not always the easiest to deal with, and the Kingman Review served to pile the pressure on the embattled regulator. Though the Government took the decision, on the back of the Review, to do away with the FRC and replace it with ARGA, the FRC still had to focus its attention on making sure the new Stewardship Code was designed appropriately, and now must steer the new Code through the early phases of its life, all whilst the concept of a Stewardship Code is under intense scrutiny.

In this chapter we will start by reviewing the Code itself. This will allow us then to move forward and assess the notable differences between this and the previous Codes. Unsurprisingly, the new Code brings with it a myriad of intricacies which are all important, but when added together present significant challenges for the future of Stewardship. If we also add to this that the FRC has widely extended the scope of the new Code, then the stakes cannot be higher for the new Code, the regulator tasked with establishing it, and the new regulator that will be tasked with taking the Code forward.

As we shall see, with the FRC extending the Code's focus, the number of issues that are associated with the concept of stewardship have been extended also. By way of preparing for the final chapter, we will touch

D. Cash and R. Goddard, *Investor Stewardship and the UK Stewardship Code*, https://doi.org/10.1007/978-3-030-87152-9_4

upon key issues in this chapter such as the legal constraints on fiduciaries when engaging in actions that may not, necessarily, be absolutely in the interests of their clients/principals. We will also ask the question of how the reports of the signatories to the new Code will be, or perhaps should be assessed. There was a massive focus in the last Code on what Kingman called 'boilerplate' reporting i.e. reports that were minimal in information and could simply be copied over into future reporting cycles. Even before one reads the new Code, it is obvious that trying to prevent such standards of reporting will be key for the new Code's success, so we shall analyse them as we go through.

Ultimately, the new Code and its aims bring forward into the light some serious issues in the modern world of investing, finance, and general business practices. There is plenty of debate on these intricacies and they are all worth assessing (which we will), but the reality is that the proposed vision of business as being *sustainable* and *responsible* means that a number of entrenched understandings within the capitalist structure will need to change. Therefore, the new Stewardship Code arguably stands as a fantastic case study which can highlight just how far the world has come since the degeneration associated with the Financial Crisis.

4.2 The New Code

Immediately, the FRC address the issue that perhaps defined the previous Codes when they start by providing a definition of Stewardship upon which the new Code is built:

> Stewardship is the responsible allocation, management and oversight of capital to create long-term value for clients and beneficiaries leading to sustainable benefits for the economy, the environment and society.[1]

The introduction endeavours to provide context to this new definition. It makes clear that the Code does not prescribe a single approach to effective stewardship and that the growth of the investment market since the last Code means there are multiple avenues to achieving the stated goals of the Code. Interestingly, the FRC acknowledge the wider implications for good stewardship and hint at what is to come in relation to the wider context of the Code:

> Environmental, particularly climate change, and social factors, in addition to governance, have become material issues for investors to consider when making investment decisions and undertaking stewardship. The Code also recognises that asset owners and asset managers play an important role as guardian of market integrity and in working to minimise systemic risks as well as being stewards of the investments in their portfolios.[2]

On one hand, this sentiment of an acknowledgement of the wider impact of poor stewardship is of course a positive sign. However, this really should have been the overriding sentiment to the first Codes, not this third iteration. Also, there are so many factors to the investment dynamic that simply prescribing that investors play an important role in the integrity of the market and systemic risk is not particularly accurate nor helpful; there is no mention here of a regulatory framework that should be in place in a properly functioning marketplace.

This potential 'disconnect' is perhaps evidenced by the final version of the definition having been changed significantly from what was proposed within the FRC's consultative process. The FRC's original definition of 'Stewardship is the responsible allocation and management of capital across the institutional investment community to create sustainable value for beneficiaries, the economy and society' proved to be controversial. In the pre-2020 Code consultation, and a joint FCA/FRC consultation, more than half of respondents were adamant that the primary purpose of stewardship is to deliver financial returns for one's client/principal.[3] This unease was arguably reflected in the finalised version of the definition, whereby wider benefits from good stewardship are to be derived from the main focus of creating long-term value for clients and beneficiaries, rather than the two being independent.[4]

Whilst some have suggested that the increased focus on climate change is a natural progression for investors who, increasingly, hold stakes in firms that have an increasing exposure to climate-related issues,[5] the reality is that the UK Government has sought, via the FRC, to co-opt the investment industry as a way of pressurising corporate managers to focus more on climate risk; this links neatly to the UK's signature on the Paris Climate Accord and its aim to be a net-zero carbon economy by 2050.[6] A question remains as to whether this is a potentially successful approach, rather than directly regulating to similar ends. There are advantages and disadvantages associated with the usage of soft law, and it appears the UK is embarking upon a subtle approach to changing the culture within its business environment. We await to see if this strategy will be effective in the long-term, but the new 2020 Code is not alone in attempting to integrate ESG into soft-law approaches.[7]

Nevertheless, the Code takes a much more expansive approach to its task this time around. Suggestions of a re-purposed but old set of principles can no longer be attributed to the UK's Stewardship Code. This is now a purpose-built Code developed in consultation with the industries the FRC (and also the FCA) regulate. This is positive. It also serves to add to the pressure placed upon the new Code, but we shall return to that later. For now, it is important to review the new set of principles.

4.2.1 A New Set of Principles

One substantial change that is immediately visible is that now the Code contains principles for service providers within the investment chain. For asset owners and asset managers, there are 12 principles, and for service providers there are 6 (Table 4.1):

As you can see, the Code splits the different Principles into groups, with Principles 1–5 focusing on the core purpose and internal governance of asset managers and owners, for example. It is worth noting that the focus on these fundamental elements mirrors the introduction of the same concepts within the UK's Corporate Governance Code.[9] Principle 2 aims to require signatories to explain how their governance processes translate into increased accountability and oversight over effective stewardship within their organisation, whilst Principle 3 self-evidently requires signatories to explain the measures taken to reduce the effect of conflicts of interest. However, in Principle 4 we see the introduction of new concepts to the concept of a Stewardship Code. The new focus on considering the systemic effects of good (and alternatively poor) stewardship is firstly represented by the (subjective) requirement that signatories demonstrate how they are promoting the concept of promoting well-functioning markets.[10] Then, with Principle 5, we see the importance of confirming and legitimising all of the above with the reviewing and assurance of the processes and the disclosures.

Principles 6–8 show an attempt by the FRC to address the relationship between parties within the investment chain. There is now a heavy

Table 4.1 Principles[8]

Principles for asset owners and asset managers	*Principles for service providers*
Purpose and Governance	1. Purpose strategy and culture
1. Purpose, strategy and culture	2. Governance, resources and incentives
2. Governance, resources and incentives	3. Conflicts of interest
3. Conflicts of interest	4. Promoting well-functioning markets
4. Promoting well-functioning markets	5. Supporting client's and stewardship
5. Review and Assurance	6. Review and Assurance
Investment Approach	
6. Client and beneficiary needs	
7.Stewardship, investment and ESG integration	
8. Monitoring managers and service providers	
Engagement	
9. Engagement	
10. Collaboration	
11. Escalation	
Exercising Rights and Responsibilities	
12.Exercising rights and responsibilities	

emphasis on signatories reporting, essentially, the health of their relationship with others, particularly beneficiaries. Not only does the inherent focus on the interests of one's beneficiaries (theoretically speaking) now need to be articulated, but the manner in which information is gathered and used now needs to be articulated also. To complete that informational cycle, the monitoring of managers and service providers injects more responsibility into the process, presumably aiming to correct some cultural issues which could prevent progression in the field i.e. increased transparency in all areas are seen as being positive for beneficiaries, but also the market as a whole. These Principles, particularly Principle 7, represent quite a change in approach for the new Code, with previous Codes concerned with what happened *after* an investment i.e. engagement, rather than the processes utilised in the lead-up to an investment.

Engagement is still a key factor, however. Principles 9 to 11 reiterate the obligations seen in past Codes regarding the role of a signatory after an investment. Whilst not calling for traditional 'activism', the Code is calling for more action to be taken by signatories where appropriate. This is why we also see reference to 'collaboration' and 'escalation', so that shareholders are encouraged to work together to push for better management where appropriate, and that issues be escalated appropriately rather than having shareholders 'walk'. This is supported by the last Principle for signatories in that one's rights and responsibilities both need to be exercised and honoured if the company is to be controlled correctly.

What is clear is that the wider emphasis of the Code is fundamentally represented within the Principles. There is now a much wider social responsibility placed upon signatories. The inclusion of new aspects such as increasing transparency crucially alters the composition and overall feel of the new Stewardship Code. The obligations have been raised. More is now being asked of signatories with the underlying sentiment being that a more present shareholder can contribute to a more effective and less-negatively-impactful financial system. It perhaps demonstrate the importance of developing a bespoke Code rather than re-purposing an older set of principles (i.e. like the ISC Principles).

4.2.2 *Differences from the 2012 Stewardship Code*

It is expected that in the eight years that passed between the 2012 and 2020 versions of the Code, that a lot would have changed. When we consider that the FRC was chastised for rushing through the development of the 2010 Code and missing a chance to make a real impact, it is not surprising that there would have been substantial changes to the new Code.

The changes have been labelled as 'substantial', with the (then) Chair of the FRC Steven Dingemans remarking that the new Code 'marks a step-change in the expectations for investors, their advisers and how they manage investments for their savers and pensioners. It is an ambitious revision that strengthens the UK's standards of governance, transparency and clear reporting'.[11] It has been argued that the new Code 'raises the bar significantly' in five particular ways:

1. Pushing signatories to take account of ESG factors in their investment decision-making processes;
2. Pushing signatories to focus on their purpose, values, and culture. The move to push signatories to *explain* their purpose, beliefs, strategies, and values is seen as a big improvement rather than just stating support of an ideal;
3. The extension of focus beyond that of asset managers is seen as a massive leap forward. Asset owners, and now service providers allow for a wider surface area upon which the ideals of good stewardship can be absorbed;
4. Pushing for further transparency from signatories. The requirement for a signatory to report annually on aspects such as voting records is seen as an improvement, although we should question how that is much different from previous versions;
5. To push for the demonstration of stewardship beyond listed equity. This is regarded as a massive change in sentiment from the regulator. Having to explain how one has pursued stewardship principles across asset classes, as well as investments outside of the UK, is seen as placing real responsibility on the targets of the Code.[12]

Others are not as 'bowled over' with the new Code, but Davies' summation that 'the FRC doubled down on its bets: it is now committed to producing a code which operates not only effectively but also over a much broader set of stewardship goals than previously'[13] is difficult to argue with; the FRC has nailed its colours to the mast. We can speculate as to whether this is because they really do not have anything left to lose with the impending disbandment coming their way, but the outcome is still the same. Davies makes the shrewd observation that in the previous Codes, engagement was key. Now, non-engagement principles outweigh engagement-related principles 8–4. He concludes by saying that 'something is clearly going on beyond the initial concept of stewardship as engagement'.[14] It is difficult to define what that something is, but a cynic may suggest that the regulatory disconnect that commonly exists in financial regulation—where regulations that look good in theory are applied to a practical environment in which it is not appropriate—has been realised; institutional investors really do have little incentive to actively engage with their investee companies, and it is not through a lack of care for the most part. It can come down to cold hard economics sometimes, and that can be very compelling (we will look again in more detail at the position of institutional investors in the next chapter).

Another change which is prevalent is the focus on annual reporting. It is theoretically important to place pressure on the signatories to report every year on how they are complying with the Code, both in practice but also in spirit. There is now a massive emphasis on embodying the sentiment of the Code and aligning one's culture to the objective of promoting long-term interests. In theory, this makes sense. But, in practice, there is the potential for this requirement to create an opposing outcome. Signatories to the Code will likely already be reporting on their stewardship efforts every year in their annual reports anyway. What the new Code is perhaps doing is forcing signatories to report in more detail. One important suggestion has been that this requirement will detract from the efforts to push signatories to think of the long-term actions of their investment strategies etc., and instead focus on reportable events each year.[15] It is therefore questionable as to whether there exists enough leeway for a signatory to adopt, say, a multi-year strategy relating to its stewardship if they have to provide solid and detailed reports every year. Will a signatory be, essentially, penalised for having little to report on their annual report to the FRC because they are in the early stages of, say, a 10-year strategy? Will the detail of that strategy be enough for the signatory to be recognised as practising good stewardship?

However, perhaps the biggest development has been in the perspective of the Code. No longer is there a narrow focus on forcing investors to engage with their investee companies, but now there is a focus on the impact of companies upon society. Additionally, the UK Government's focus on climate change is fundamentally incorporated into the fibres of the new Code. Whilst the aim seems to be the mainstreaming of the concept of ESG, there are political dynamics at play which are affecting the Code's chances of succeeding. In pushing investors to consider the wider impacts of the companies they are invested in, Fisch argues that the Code is trying to consider investors as shareholders, and no longer as intermediaries.[16] This may well be the case, but the reality is that the Government are now tasking the private sector with protecting against systemic risk, all via a soft-law regime. This is controversial to say the least, particularly when we consider the underlying dynamics that negatively affect the chances of institutional shareholders engaging with their investee companies. Davies very slightly intimates at an 'invisible hand' from the UK State, whereby the reputational risk for an investor or company of not complying with the ESG-focused push is not just reputational, but all operating under the substantial shadow of hard law being implemented in the field so that 'asset owners and managers, it is argued, will want to keep regulation at bay in order to protect their business models and that will require doing enough in relation to ESG considerations to keep the government happy'.[17] He augments this argument by comparing to the experience of the UK Takeover Code, and suggests that the new Stewardship Code may have more success and continue to move forward, as long as the looming threat of hard law is maintained by the Government.

This is perhaps why it is easy to highlight the changes that have been made but exceptionally difficult to predict the impact that they will have. The Stewardship Code sits in the middle of a delicate tug-of-war between the private and public sector, and the political approach of the Conservative Party (the party currently leading the UK Government) is currently adopting the sentiment of believing in the private sector to 'do good'. It will be interested to see if (ever) there will be a time when the Government's hand is called and the sole question becomes whether a British Government will take the decision to directly intervene in the practice of private investment, which would be quite the departure from traditional sentiment.

4.2.3 *Major Issues That Have Already Been Revealed*

There have been a number of issues with the new Code that the field have already identified. A number of those issues will be focused on more in the final chapter so we will only briefly hint at them here, but they are all significant.

The first, which is something we will go into much more detail in the next chapter, is the concept of assurance. Assurance in this field relates to a party verifying the contents of a given piece of information so that others can rely on its content (very simply put). Assurance, therefore, is of crucial importance in relation to both Stewardship and also compliance with the Stewardship Code. If the information within a given disclosure is not accurate, inflated, misrepresented, or even just erroneous, the users of that information should be able to rely on a process that identifies those issues before they receive it. This is why it is disappointing to read, in the Code itself, that 'the FRC cannot provide assurance' for the disclosures of the regulated targets.[18] However, the Code does state, in Principle 5, that signatories should review their policies and the effectiveness of these policies, and then declare what assurance—whether internal or external—they have procured. The Code states that 'internal assurance may be given by senior staff, a designated body, board, committee, or internal audit and external assurance by an independent third party'.[19] So, whilst the concept of having such declarations assured is noted within the Code, any sort of consistency or industry-wide standards for this are not present. It remains to be seen whether such flexibility will have negative effects in the eyes of the users of the declared reports.

Flexibility is often a gift and a curse when it comes to business. On the one hand, increased flexibility allows for business to be proactive, able to respond quickly, and able to maximise one's position in ways that suit their particular business model/strategy/position etc. On the other hand, flexibility does not lend itself to setting standards. When we consider the concept of assurance for example, who is to say what can be trusted? Will an investor or company be penalised in the eyes of the field for only internally assuring, for example? One element of the Code where flexibility has the potential to be really damaging is in the interpretation of what is—and cue the dreaded word—*material*. The concept of materiality has, is, and likely will continue to plague the integration of ESG into mainstream business practices and in relation to stewardship it appears to be no different. Davies suggests that 'given the uncertainties around the empirical data, it is likely that pension fund trustees (and asset owners subject to similar duties) will have a significant discretion in this area, providing they act in good faith and remain within conventional views about the financial values of pursuing ESG policies'.[20] This relates to another concept that massively impacts the integration of ESG—fiduciary duties—which we will cover more in the next chapter, but the flexibility that will seemingly be afforded to trustees and asset owners belies a fundamental issue that is yet to be resolved in the world of ESG. Perhaps it is merely a question of timing, but the reality is that the concept of ESG is being pushed into the mainstream business arena, likely, before it has had chance to be fundamentally tested and accepted. There is, in that sense, an argument to be had that the pushing of ESG needs to come before the acceptance. However, there is an underlying risk that business will pay lip-service to the concept, because it is being pushed, but do not absolutely buy into it. This is probably rational. In that sense then, it is right to give business the flexibility to decide what is material and what is not. Yet, the impact of a lack of standard regarding what is material, why, and for how long, potentially inhibits the true development of ESG as a concept. It has been argued that ESG, and the concept of 'responsible' or 'sustainable' business can never truly be 'mainstreamed' because of the plurality of underlying tension in the vast arena that is 'business'.[21] If a concept a. has to be forced, and b. cannot by design apply to the majority within a field, the question becomes just how successful can it be?

Another issue is whether the new Code has the tools to succeed where its predecessor failed, in that it needs to provide asset owners and managers the reasoning and rationale to 'extract themselves, through stewardship reporting, from potential destructive short-term, share value-driven decision-making, or that there is a sufficient incentive for them to become increasingly active for the long-term success of the company'.[22] Muchlinksi questions the potential success of this, noting that the first two Codes did not even come close. One way of disciplining the market has been for the FRC to adopt a 'tiering process', which describes a system whereby signatories are essentially named-and-shamed depending on the quality of their disclosure and reporting. In the new regime, an entity either becomes a signatory or they do not, with the FRC deciding on allowing alignment with the Code based upon the quality of submission. This has the potential to lead to costs of compliance for the marketplace, which has the further potential of market leaders taking the lead and having their submissions accepted, and then others waiting and copying their submission framework once what is required becomes clearer after the first round of reporting—all to save cost.[23] The first round of reporting will therefore be crucial to the development of the Code, and there have been suggestions that all is not well on that front.

4.3 Early Signs

With a new Code such as the Stewardship Code, and particularly the rate of difference in relation to the previous Codes, it is to be expected that there will be teething problems. To combat this, the FRC produced a Report in September 2020 that detailed the quality of a small selection of early submissions, and provided guidance as to what went well and what could be improved. This will be helpful for the early signatories and the momentum that the new Code surely needs to generate in light of the pressure it is under.

The FRC analysed 21 early submissions and analysed them against the 12 main principles. Although the majority of the Reports came from Asset

Managers, the FRC was at pains to make clear that the review would be relevant to all potential signatories. Perhaps it comes down to perspective—i.e. whether a. there should have been a high rate of compliance and good reporting because prospective signatories have been involved more in the design of the new Code and also profess to do much of what the Code asks for anyway, or b. anything new like this will always require room for manoeuvre in the early stages and that this should be expected—but the reality has been that 'the FRC finds varying degrees of quality in the documents it reviewed'.[24]

There were two key outcomes. The first was that the FRC found that very few covered all 12 principles in their submission. There was also a lack of cross-referencing on show, which the FRC would like to see more of so that signatories demonstrate they understand that the principles do not sit in isolation. The second element that stood out was that where a reporting expectation does not apply, the FRC found that there was a tendency to ignore it, rather than explain why there has been no explanation given. Some in the field have suggested that a number of the conditions in the new Code require meaningful and potentially longer-term reflection, so there may be a bit of a lag whilst signatories truly get to grips with the concept of the new Stewardship Code and what it is aiming to achieve.[25]

However, whilst there are some negative elements in the early reporting, there are a range of positives. There has been a clear attempt to engage with the new Code, and it may just be the case that what is expected of signatories can only be truly refined by such a trial-and-error process. The FRC did make constant reference to the variety of reporting,[26] which can potentially be explained by the lack of a standard being prescribed by the Code itself, but also of the flexible sentiment the Code has been pushing in its new guise. The guidance from the FRC is helpful in many ways, but in some ways not. For example, some chose to submit on a principle-by-principle basis, and some did not—the FRC simply said 'we saw effective examples of both approaches'.[27] It is difficult to tell what exactly the FRC is looking for and, as such, the scenario we mentioned earlier whereby there will be early adopters who, as a result of being confirmed as a signatory by the FRC, will then be copied by others. Although the early adopters may see no other choice or have calculated that the benefits outweigh the costs, there is a cost imbalance at play here akin to the concept of a 'free rider'.

What was of interest before we finish the chapter was that key elements that the FRC left to the market to sort out have not, unsurprisingly, been addressed. For example, the key issue of assurance and who will verify the information was noted by the FRC as being 'one of the weaker principles in the reports that we reviewed and a few reports did not refer to it all'.[28] This argument will be revisited in the next chapter, but the FRC really have made a rod for their own back here. In not prescribing a standard for assurance, or even hinting at one, the lack of effort by signatories reveals the Achilles heel of the new Code—if the information cannot, or will not be assured, then can it be relied upon? Will this reality merely just translate into a more detailed boilerplate reporting fiasco that overshadowed the last Codes? It is questionable how standards can be applied to the issue of assurance in the stewardship realm, but the lack of analysis and/or prescription of at least some sort of standard is troublesome for the new Code, and the early responses have raised an alarm bell in that regard.

4.4 Conclusion

It is difficult to know whether the Stewardship Code 2020 is an evolution of the previous Codes, or a revolution. It is perhaps a revolution in some ways because the emphasis has changed so dramatically. Gone is the (probably misguided) focus on engagement and in its place a call for market participants to take much more responsibility for systemic issues. The integral incorporation now of ESG suggests that the FRC see the Stewardship Code 2020 as a vehicle within which ESG can be mainstreamed into the British business consciousness.

These are no small feats. If we consider the Stewardship Code 2020 to be under incredible pressure because it is potentially ' now or never' for the concept of a soft-law-based Stewardship Code, then such large ambitions may have one of two outcomes. If the objectives of further mainstreaming ESG and forcing market participants to think systemically are achieved, then the concept of soft-law guidance for the markets will not only be maintained, but fundamentally strengthened in the UK. However, if the new Code does not meet its objective, then the lingering shadow of hard law may be forced to translate into action. This is extremely problematic, because one can only speculate to the level of appetite for State intervention in the investment practices of private investors. Yes, there are many instances of more forceful State intervention in private matters, but private investment lies at the very heart of modern capitalism and enforcing nonfinancial principles upon private entities seems to be lightyears away from the reality of the modern marketplace. It has already been suggested in the British press that the Stewardship Code 2020, even with all of its flexibility, could 'stop firms listing in the UK',[29] so the impact of even more intervention could be massively impactful, and likely in a negative manner. In a post-Brexit UK scrambling for global appeal, the writing may be on the wall and the looming threat of hard-law may just be that, a looming threat and nothing more. The question is then whether market participants will ever get close to calling their bluff.

What the Stewardship Code 2020 does, for a number of reasons, is draw a line in the sand. This marks the end of the FRC-era and leads us into the ARGA-era. The systemic focus of the new Code perhaps details for us a focus from regulators on private entities taking the leading in shaping the new, hopefully more sustainable business future. There can be debate on the efficacy of that approach. But what we do know is that the new Code pushes the boundary more than the old Codes. This was not as rushed or reactive as the 2010 Code and, as such, the FRC have nowhere to hide. This is a good thing. The increase in pressure all around is a positive factor in producing impact. Early reporting has shown green shoots which can be nurtured, but yet again (as always) there are clear signs of the misalignment between regulatory theory and business practice. The allowance for flexibility has translated itself into opportunity to show noncompliance. This was always going to be the case. The hope is now that the early bumps-in-the-road which, admittedly, are not the greatest of obstacles, can be smoothed out so that the majority of the field have a greater understanding of what is required, but more crucially *why*. It is clear from the FRC's responses to early submissions that the *why* is now equally as important as the *what*—we now get to see whether the field truly believes in the concept of stewardship, long-term business principles, and perhaps to a lesser form the true meaning and aim of ESG integration. There are a number of aspects which ARGA must grapple with it if it is to successfully evolve the Stewardship Code as the financial arena continue to adapt to the Covid-19 pandemic. The in-tray for ARGA is a substantial one indeed.

Notes

1. Financial Reporting Council, *The UK Stewardship Code 2020* (FRC 2020) https://www.frc.org.uk/getattachment/5aae591d-d9d3-4cf4-814a-d14e156a1d87/Stewardship-Code_Dec-19-Final-Corrected.pdf, 4.
2. Ibid.
3. Financial Reporting Council, *Proposed Revision to the UK Stewardship Code* (2019) https://www.frc.org.uk/getattachment/8caa0e9c-58bb-41b2-923e-296223755174/Consultation-on-Proposed-Revisions-to-the-UK-Stewardship-Code-Jan-2019.pdf.
4. Paul L Davies, 'The UK Stewardship Code 2010–2010: From Saving the Company to Saving the Planet?' (2020) ECGI Working Paper Series 506/2020 25.
5. Asset Management Taskforce, *Investing with Purpose: Placing Stewardship at the Heart of Sustainable Growth* (2020) https://www.theia.org/sites/default/files/2020-11/Asset%20Management%20Taskforce_proof7.pdf.
6. Davies (n 4) 28.
7. Dionysia Katelouzou and Alice Klettner, 'Sustainable Finance and Stewardship: Unlocking Stewardship's Sustainability' (2020) ECGI Working Paper 521/2020 20.
8. FRC (n 1) 2.
9. FRC, The UK Corporate Governance Code, July 2018, Principle 1: Board Leadership and Company Purpose.
10. FRC (n 1) 4.
11. Steve Giles, 'The Five Most Important Changes to the UK's New Stewardship Code' (2020) ACCA Global (January 1) https://www.accaglobal.com/in/en/member/discover/cpd-articles/governance-risk-control/stewardship-codecpd.html.
12. Ibid.
13. Davies (n 4) 5.
14. Ibid 7.
15. Ibid 22.
16. Jill E Fisch, 'The Uncertain Stewardship Potential of Index Funds' (2020) ECGI Working Paper 490/2020 https://poseidon01.ssrn.com/delivery.php?ID=192119095117089121120086127093071027037049067002004033093113121127111092093081086073055124012115006097026113091086073127029098018034038013029070065021018127114006080032014003066080006064114105007028120073010098123070099071079110118072029109091084085029&EXT=pdf&INDEX=TRUE.
17. Davies (n 4) 31.
18. FRC (n 1) 30.
19. Ibid 12.

20. Davies (n 4) 26.
21. Daniel Cash, *Sustainable Rating Agencies vs Credit Rating Agencies: The Battle to Serve the Mainstream Investor* (Palgrave Macmillan 2021).
22. Peter Muchlinksi, *Multinational Enterprises and the Law* (OUP 2021) 366.
23. Jimmie Franklin, 'Primer: The UK Stewardship Code' (2020) *International Financial Law Review* (June 19).
24. Jimmie Franklin, 'FRC Review of Early Stewardship Code Reports Highlights Areas for Improvement' (2020) 402 *Occupational Pensions* 6.
25. Franklin (n 23).
26. Financial Reporting Council, *The UK Stewardship Code: Review of Early Reporting —September 2020* (FRC 2020) https://www.frc.org.uk/getattachment/975354b4-6056-43e7-aa1f-c76693e1c686/The-UK-Stewardship-Code-Review-of-Early-Reporting.pdf.
27. Ibid 5.
28. Ibid 24.
29. Emily Gosden, 'Stewardship Code Could 'Stop Firms Listing in UK' (2019) *The Times* (May 29).

CHAPTER 5

The Future of Stewardship

5.1 Introduction

The future of the concept of Stewardship, in the UK at least, will perhaps be guided by how a number of important and connected issues play out. How the FRC and the new ARGA regulator operates with regards to the new Code is also important. The new Stewardship Code arguably represents a pinch-point in the development of the concept in the UK. The first Code and its quick revision were clearly built on weak and reactionary foundations. This new Code has been built in consultation with the field, in plenty of time, and from a wider perspective. The key question is however whether it can be any more effective. There have been teething problems in the early stages of reporting, but that can be expected. The key will be how, once the first stage of reporting is officially over, the Code has influenced not only reporting, but crucially how it has affected practice.

The wider scope of the Code and its wider objectives relating to systemic issues are, on one hand, to be lauded. It is clear that, to a certain extent, bringing on board private corporate actors can be a key element to achieving such systemically important goals (like positively affecting climate change etc.) Yet, on the other hand, there is a fine balance to be found, and it is questionable as to whether the Code has found that balance. Placing all the responsibility on private corporate actors, in a

D. Cash and R. Goddard, *Investor Stewardship and the UK Stewardship Code*, https://doi.org/10.1007/978-3-030-87152-9_5

soft-law voluntary manner, is arguably misguided at best and irresponsible at worst. With the incredible number of different factors underlying the stewardship dynamic, the position of the Code is a very tentative one indeed. When we add to this that there is pressure on the Code to get it right in a 'now or never' manner, and also a changing of the regulatory guard during its early life, then the stakes are indeed high for this latest iteration of the UK Stewardship Code.

As we look to the future of Stewardship, we focus on three key issues that we believe will affect the development of stewardship either way. Those are: the concept of 'fiduciary duties' and how they interact with the concept of stewardship; the concept of 'assurance' within the stewardship field and how that may (need) to progress; and finally the development of the new regulator ARGA and how they may seek to regulate the field with their new powers. There are of course other factors that may affect the development of Stewardship, but these three elements will be highly impactful. Another element that we will add in this final chapter is a focus on the position of the institutional investor. The reason we do this is because it is quite clear, having reviewed a number of regulatory initiatives, that the concept of regulatory misalignment could be alive and well in the arena of stewardship regulation. Understanding the inherent dynamics affecting the regulated position is fundamental for successful regulation, and we have seen on multiple occasions instances of where that crucial understanding has been missing (Banking, auditor, and credit rating regulation come to mind but there are so many more). Therefore, we will end with a short review of this position so as to demonstrate the potential of co-opting institutional investors into the curing of systemic problems.

5.2 The Fiduciary Disconnect

One of the key aspects to the new Code is that it is fundamentally possible to do good business, and also do good. The focus on expanding the scope of responsibility of shareholders is perhaps the key change to the new Code.[1] In the Code there is no mention of any conflict between these two positions. However, in practice, the approach has not been well received. In the FRC's own consultation[2] and the joint FCA/FRC consultation,[3] the approach proved to be controversial. Respondents, many of whom were, of course, institutional investors, signified clearly that they believe the primary purpose of stewardship, as a concept, is to focus on the returns of their clients.[4] The argument, traditionally, is that focusing on other aspects is fine as long as they are 'material' to the primary objective of generating returns. Proponents of this argument argue, with the backing of the law, that they have a *fiduciary duty* to put these financial interests of their clients above all else. This new Code challenges that perception, fundamentally. The argument now is whether considering aspects such as ESG aspects is actually a part of one's fiduciary duties as it has, as the argument goes, a *material* effect on the position of the beneficiaries. As a result, the original proposed version of the Code had to be amended to now suggest that the benefits to those outside of one's beneficiaries are by-products, and not objectives.[5]

This conflict between what constitutes one's fiduciary duties has been, is, and will continue to be perhaps the central cause for tension in the development of the mainstreamisation of 'stewardship'. There have been attempts to clarify the importance of adding nonfinancial consideration into the traditional concept of fiduciary duties—like the Law Commission[6]—but there has been little progress. Studies of market participants have found that, generally, there is still a lot of confusion.[7] Ultimately, there have been no legal developments forcing the changing of the traditional understanding of both a. what fiduciary duty means in the modern context, and b. how that would even be applied.

The applicability of considering ESG when undertaking investment decisions and stewardship activities are, of course, very different. There is evidence that considering ESG in one's stewardship activities can help with understanding the performance of investments and funds,[8] but ultimately the question still centres on the issue of materiality. The issue has been considered in the literature and a differentiation has been suggested to be that considering nonfinancial information, for example, could be a breach of one's fiduciary duties if they are done in the interests of others (say, the public) rather than one's beneficiaries.[9] It appears that the 'benefits' of stewardship activities for the public must be a by-product of one's stewardship, otherwise those in charge of an asset owner or manager could find themselves liable. The only argument that could allow such an integration of something other than purely financial consideration is that whatever one was considering, say something related to ESG, was in the *long-term* interest of one's beneficiaries.[10]

Perhaps, then, the most important issue is the materiality of ESG and other nonfinancial considerations. If it can be proven that considering ESG, for example, is a benefit to one's beneficiaries then there is no issue.

It might not be the case that this is difficult to prove, but that it is difficult to align to the traditional time horizons we see at play within the investment chain. The financial materiality of ESG issues has, for the most part, been confirmed although not universally.[11]Considering ESG information can help an investor with their longer-term portfolio decisions i.e. on whether to exclude or divest,[12] but the reality is that beneficiaries can be advantaged by a manager or owner engaging proactively with their stewardship activities based upon ESG information. If an asset manager, for example, believes that engaging better with a company to improve their impact upon the environment would bear fruit in the future (say, on their market share for example) then there is arguably an obligation to conduct that proactive approach. Another issue then is just how one quantifies the concept of benefit for the beneficiaries, particularly when the action may take years to transform into a result. Again, the issue of time horizons is crucial.[13]

One of the most recent large reports on this area was developed by the Principles for Responsible Investment (PRI) initiative. The PRI, in 2019, examined the global picture with regards to how fiduciary duties are viewed, and the factors affecting the concept's progression.[14] Whilst the Report set out a wide body of evidence to show that ESG issues do have financial materiality, the conclusion was that the interrelationship between investment and sustainability is still one-sided. For example, one's fiduciary duties will dictate that a manager, for example must consider the sustainability impact upon an investment, but not the investment's impact upon the concept of sustainability.[15]

The sentiment of the report is that there needs to be a coherent consideration of more than just the financial return on investment. Considering the impact upon an investment of, say, environmental issues is, the PRI argue, only half the battle. This, just like the arguments regarding whether asset owners/managers have a fiduciary duty to consider nonfinancial aspects in their stewardship approach, is all based on the primacy of the financial return. In reality, if the wider picture is not considered e.g., the protection of the environment, there will not be any financial returns in the future anyway. The identified issue is that true long-term thinking encompasses many different contexts, not just the financial one. Until this is resolved in favour of a wider scope, the argument (and maybe defence) of one having a fiduciary duty to consider financial return above all else will continue to be witnessed (and used).

5.2.1 Way Forward

It is impossible for a asset owner or manager to get everything right with the deployment of funds that stem from others. However, fiduciary duties to do not aim for perfection. They aim for standards of conduct and to instil a culture of honesty, integrity, and service. The law, with regards to the duties of those in a fiduciary position, has been developed in the UK for quite some while. The culture that the law has attempted to build is a honesty-based culture that promotes the position of the beneficiary. The way this has been done has been to align it with modern capitalist or economic principles regarding the primacy of financial return. This is why we are hearing so many responses from those in a fiduciary position that to deviate from that established culture risks their position and puts them in legal jeopardy (which breaching one's fiduciary duties does indeed do).

If the culture of a fiduciary duty has been developed and established, it stands to reason that another culture could be developed or, better still, the current culture could be evolved. If the law was to amend its position to say that one's fiduciary duties *should* include the consideration of x, y, or z, then the culture would indeed develop. For example, it could be declared by law that ESG considerations *must* be considered in every investment action. However, that technically equates to the public intervention in private matters, and that is particularly contentious in the modern era, and particularly in the UK.

There have been suggestions to relax or even expand the duties for those in a fiduciary role.[16] There has also been calls for the law to be reconsidered and adapted to the modern environment. Alternatively, development in this area could be achieved by the issue being raised in a Court of Law, like that witnessed in Australia recently.[17] However, this again is a public entity (the judiciary, and in England and Wales at least an unelected one) intervening in private matters. When we additionally understand that this would be an intervention in the role of a trustee, then the stakes are raised even further and almost to a prohibitive level—it is hard to imagine a government, or a member of the judiciary, who would have the appetite to dictate to trustees in furtherance of the legal constraints already placed upon them. For the markets to survive, there has to be at least some modicum of independence and intervention at this level could severely hamper that.

There is also ambiguity, flexibility, and plurality in the area of Fiduciary Duty. Reisberg and Tilba tell us that the concept is 'highly flexible, loose, and uncertain'. The 'plurality of fiduciary duty interpretations' as the scholars call it, suggests that finding a base standard will be difficult. This means that, moving forward, there is plenty of scope for institutional investors (inclusive of the wide scope that can be classed as such) to revert back to their duties, *as they see them*, and make the point as to why they are not considering ESG up to a particular level. The effect of this could be that the calls for standard setting in this arena, and for the pursuing of an industry-wide push towards ESG and nonfinancial integration, could be falling on deaf ears for a while. However, it is has been said by the Law Commission no less that 'it would not make sense to say that trustees must take an ESG approach'.[18] Similarly, it has been strongly argued that institutional investors 'should not be seen as unpaid, unelected agents of public policy'.[19] One wonders if this is why, in the Stewardship Code 2020, the word 'fiduciary' is not mentioned once.

The idea to bring in private actors, who have legal duties to consider their clients and beneficiaries, into a societal role is a difficult one to achieve. Pension Fund trustees have already spoken of how they feel, under the new societal push, that they are being asked to consider the position of the companies they invest in *above* that of the pensioners they are tasked with protecting.[20] This is clearly at odds with their mandate. The system is now asking them to do more than their original mandate, although they are only tentatively asking them to at this stage. There are rules creeping in, and the shadow of hard law grows ever larger, but for the investors there are a number of factors pulling at their position. One thing that could really push things along is that, on top of the research that suggests that ESG consideration is economically useful, there could be more reliability in the system as a whole with regards to both the ESG information within the field, the declarations of the investee companies, and also the stewardship efforts of the investors. To do that, we need to look at the concept of assurance.

5.3 The Importance (and Risk) of Assurance

We have touched upon the concept of assurance earlier in the book. In the Stewardship Code 2020, the FRC declare that they will not be able to provide assurance for the information submitted under the new Code. They instead state, in Principle 5, that it is the responsibility of the signatory to provide assurance, and that they can do this either internally, or externally via a third party. We saw at the end of the last chapter that, in reality, the early signatories have either paid this lip-service or just not done it. It will not be surprising to see others follow suit once the first full round of reporting has been completed.

There has been very little in terms of development regarding assurance within the stewardship sector. In the field of sustainability-related reporting, there has been some development; just enough to give us an insight into the concept of providing assurance for nonfinancial information. There has been plenty of research to suggest that there are theoretical advantages to having one's nonfinancial information assured, and particularly by an external third party. It will not be surprising as to why. The concept of 'information asymmetry' comes to the fore here and neatly describes the dynamic between different parties. In relation to sustainability and nonfinancial declarations, investors are pushing companies to be more sustainable and also to prove it, but have no way of being able to absolutely understand whether the company's declarations are accurate. Assurance is one of the cures for informational asymmetry.[21] The presence of a theoretically independent third party allows for a. the information to be verified, b. the company to protect commercially sensitive information but still *signal* to the market, and c. each investor to reduce their costs for having to undertake assurance on each investable entity, as now they can just bear witness to the validation of the information. We highlight the word signal here because, arguably, that is the main draw of having information assured.[22] It simply allows one party to signal to another (or many others) that what they are saying can be relied upon.

The benefits of assurance grow even further in relation to nonfinancial information. Financial information must be assured by law, which is why auditors are one of the oldest financial institutions. However, for nonfinancial information, there are two components to it which make assurance essential. The first is that it is highly subjective as to what is useful and what is not, but having information assured helps to produce confidence in the relatively novel process.[23] Second, and in relevance to what we spoke about in the last section, there is an understandable reticence aimed towards the concept of ESG, nonfinancial information, and its usefulness. Having information assured can help parties both believe in it more, and also signal to the parties they have to perform for that the actions they are taking can be relied upon as being, potentially, *material*.

With regards to stewardship, we currently have the situation where the regulator will not check the declarations made under the new Code, and it is completely up to the signatories how they assure their information (either internally or externally). The regulator will check a sample of declarations to check for consistency and improprieties, but this is not a substitute for full assurance, of course. Furthermore, it is questionable whether taking the decision not to assure at all (in any meaningful sense) will even have any consequences. We are yet to hear anything of how the Code will be enforced, apart from the threat of not being able to become a signatory. It is understandable why the regulator would not seek to provide assurance, because it will be a massively high but also unnecessary cost for a regulator that is about to be disbanded, and who is already raising its budget (to aid with the transition to ARGA) which the market participants pay for.[24] For the market participants, assurance can be costly.[25] Whilst many in the sustainability reporting field find it to be a trade-off which they are willing to pay for (increased reputational pay-off against the monetary cost),[26] the reality is that asset owners and asset managers do not have the same incentive. Perhaps if the market was less established, the competitional pressures would force asset managers to compete on the basis of being better stewards than the rest, but as we have heard a number of asset owners are concerned with their returns first, and not with the systemic risks the regulators and government would have them consider more. If an asset manager has a track record of taking care with one's money and investing wisely, then it is unlikely not being the frontrunner when it comes to Stewardship Code compliance will prove a hurdle when it comes to selecting a manager.

However, we strongly advocate for assurance to become fundamental within the concept of stewardship. The information that is submitted to the Code must be able to be relied upon. The history of boilerplate submissions and box-ticking leaves a heavy mark on the concept of stewardship reporting in the UK. This is likely why so many have suggested that it is now or never for the Stewardship Code. Assurance has all the potential to resolve this issue. However, the question then becomes will the signatories pay to have their submissions and declarations assured? There is an argument to say that the new Code missed an opportunity to set a standard and enforce assurance. Yet, there are a number of issues with this suggestion and the regulators were likely fully aware of them.

The first issue is that there is no defined international standard for nonfinancial assurance. In the field of sustainability disclosure assurance, there are many international standards which, although the different organisations are clearly trying to help, the result has been a confusing and pluralistic set of standards which puts the whole field back at square one.[27] For stewardship disclosure, the opposite is true in that the field has not even begun yet, really. If it were to be enforced now, there is no standard to align to. If there was a call to create a standard, it is likely there would be a scramble to create a standard and the result would be the same as in the sustainability reporting field.

Second, as mentioned above, assurance can be relatively costly. If it is merely being enforced to increase the reputation of the concept of stewardship then the investors would not, perhaps, be particularly receptive to incurring this extra cost when, in reality, their mission is to increase the value of their client/beneficiaries' monies. If there is not a direct and palpable incentive, it also becomes questionable whether incurring such costs would be in the best interests of one's client/beneficiary, which brings us back to the issue of one having a fiduciary duty.

Third, and perhaps most importantly, is the reality that there are fundamental issues with the concept of having a third party involved. One is that in procuring assurance services, one is deflecting the 'problem of uncertain quality of [content] to a third-party'.[28] Whilst this is a fundamental premise of third-party resolutions to informational asymmetry, there are a number of associated factors which can cause risk. What if the market for assurance of a particular sector is only young; can that assurance be trusted? If it is an established assurance service, then what competitional pressures are the service providers facing? If they are in an oligopoly for example, the pressures are radically different to say, an open market without domination. Also, who pays for the assurance? If the managers submitting stewardship reports are the ones paying for the assurance services, there is then a clear conflict of interest in terms of pressure from the manager for a good report, and pressure on the assurance provider to gain more business by providing favourable reports.

These ideas sound conspiratorial, but they are grounded in experience. It has been found in the sustainability assurance field that there can be significant managerial influence placed upon the relationship. There is also evidence on conflicts arising when assurance service providers act both as assurors and consultants.[29] Channuntapitat makes the valid argument that the independence of nonfinancial assurors stems from the independence of financial assurors (who may be the same entity, such as traditional auditors) when in reality the two environments are markedly different. The nonfinancial environment is largely unregulated, especially when compared to the financial assurance realm. This massively increases the risk of transgression. There is also the question of liability, because the liability attached to financial assurance can be substantial whilst the novelty of the nonfinancial marketplace means we do not yet know the liability parameters. This is just a further incentive for transgressive behaviour. This has been seen in other environments time and time again, as observers of the audit or credit rating industries will be quick to tell you.

At the moment, regulatory speaking, we are betwixt and between. Assurance has been requested, but almost with a shrug of the shoulders. It remains to be seen whether internal assurance will carry any weight at all. For external assurance, we will wait to find out who is selected, against what standard the information will be assured, and how the market will react to it. Maybe a new market for such service will sprout up. What we do know is that this incredibly important feature to financial or nonfinancial reporting has been relegated in the thought process of the new Code. We are of the strongest opinion that meaningful assurance should be enforced rather than suggested, and that will likely come from the professional services sector. However, this brings with it a number of risks like those identified above. Therefore, either pathway brings with it complications. Those complications will be the job of the new regulator as 2023 will soon be upon us. We wonder how that new regulator will navigate such issues.

5.4 ARGA

Admittedly, and likely unhelpfully, there is not much that we know about the new regulator. At the time of writing, the legislative agenda for the establishment of the new regulator has not even been decided.The FRC has assumed that the transition period will be extended to 2023 and is working on that basis. For the FRC, their objective now is to implement the recommendations of a number of Reviews that have taken place, and prepare for the transition. The recommendations of the Kingman Review, the Brydon Review (which considered the quality and effectiveness of audit), and the Competition and Markets Authority's Review of the statutory audit services market have all been integrated into the transitionary programme of the FRC to make the move to ARGA as smooth as possible.

To do that there are six 'workstreams'. They are:

1. Setting up the new regulator;
2. Audit scope and regulation;
3. Corporate regulation;
4. Corporate reporting;
5. Corporate governance; and
6. Market reform.

There are a number of elements within these workstreams that can only be activated via legislation—particularly setting up the new regulator as it will have a legal foundation which the FRC never had—but the FRC do state that they continue to 'work closely with the Secretary of State and BEIS to find ways to take forwards many of the recommendations without legislative changes'.[31] It has been noted that the Covid-19 pandemic has disrupted the legislative plans.[32]

Interestingly, the new regulator is being placed under pressure before it has even come into existence. For example, in a report published in March 2021, the Department for Business, Energy and Industrial Strategy (BEIS) makes clear that for the new regulator achieve the governmentally supported goal of focusing more on outcomes rather than policy statement, and identifying effectiveness and commitment, it 'will require the regulator to develop and apply a robust process for assessing the quality of signatories' reporting against the Code'.We know the FRC has said that it will not be assuring any of the information submitted, so what does this statement from BEIS mean? Does it mean that the new regulator will have to change course? Does it mean that a new standard will be developed for the field by then, potentially backed by the regulator? Or does it mean that the Government has declared something it does not understand, adding further complication to a situation where more complication is simply unhelpful? Rather than provide any guidance, the Government has instructed regulators—the FRC, the FCA, the DWP (Department of Work and Pensions), and the Pensions Regulator—to launch a review of the regulatory framework for effective stewardship, inclusive of reviewing the early success of the new Stewardship Code, in 2023. It concludes, ominously, by confirming that 'the Government will work with these bodies to determine the criteria by which the success of the Code will be measured'.[34]

The Government hint at the hard-law shadow, and the new regulator will need to deal with being placed within this political no-man's land. The Government state that:

> The Government will consider whether further powers are needed to assess and promote compliance with the Code following the outcomes of the review commenced in 2023. This could also include considering the case to amend DWP legislation or FCA and Local Government Association rules to introduce stronger requirements for reporting on the Code or to alter the balance between a rules and voluntary Code-based approach if the desired outcomes have not been achieved.[35]

This threat of a more rules-based approach is accentuated by stories from the European continent which contain details of regulators—the Danish Financial Supervisory Authority—setting up 'enforcement units' with regards to the compliance with the Sustainable Finance Disclosure Regulation that the EU has put in place.[36] Whilst not technically the same field, the concept of voluntary-based soft-law seems to be particularly under pressure. The early reports submitted to the FRC also do not help matters. The main question for the new regulator becomes, perhaps, how they may seek to enforce the Code. What happens if there are only a small number of prospective signatories who do actually assure their work properly, and answer the aspects of the Code openly and fully? Will the regulator accept having fewer signatories? Surely not. There is a 'pinch-point' coming that may not have been considered as fully as it should have been. The new regulator needs to have teeth, because the underlying sentiment of all the criticism aimed towards the FRC has been, arguably, its lack of teeth.

Though 2023 is not far away, there is plenty of time for the regulator to be built so that it can adequately meet the challenges it will surely face. The workstreams that the FRC have developed will surely help. However, what is really required to help ARGA hit the ground is regulatory cohesion from those around it. The Government really must take care with its comments, because saying things like the regulator needs to build a robust system for checking information, without any support for that massively important but hugely resource-intensive objective is foolhardy. It is crucial that the new regulator is not set up to fail with it being buoyed by regulatory inefficiency even before it starts. The initiatives put forward by institutions like BEIS and others have to be proportionate, considered, and most of all practical. An important place to start is by truly understanding those that one is to regulate.

5.5 Regulatory Alignment and Institutional Investors

We have looked at institutional investors throughout this book, so we do not want to cover old ground again here. However, it is timely here to make the point that the new regulator must understand the intricacies affecting those who it will be regulating. Too many times has a regulator, backed by legislative and political pressure, been found guilty (not literally of course) of what we call 'regulatory misalignment'. One should not be regulating those that they *want* to regulate, but only those standing in front of them to be regulated. For example, is it really a surprise to read that the early submissions to the FRC contain significant non-compliance with the need to assure the information submitted? We have only really briefly glanced at the position of the institutional investors in this short book, and already we know that there a number of reasons why the above would not be surprising. In light of the assessing the new regulator and its chances of succeeding, a quick look at the core position of the regulated may help gauge the chances of success.

Let us begin, however, with making something abundantly clear. Institutional investors, and whether one focuses on asset owners or managers, are concerned with doing right by those they are entrusted to lead. It is not suggested here, at all, that these entities are standing in the way of promoting better ideas of stewardship and contributing to a better financial system—that is simply not the case. There are some real pioneers in this area who are laudably pushing themselves to be better corporate citizens. What we are focusing on here is the structural composition that can either aid or hinder whatever reality regulators, legislators, and politicians have. So, to begin with, we would like to talk about a concept called 'rational reticence'.

As Roberts neatly describes for us:

> Institutional investors will realise little, if any, performance value from proactive exercise of their governance rights; the mobilisation costs are simply too high. Institutional investors are primarily concerned with, and specialise in, delivering comparatively superior investment performance over short periods of time, while minimizing costs and risk. Institutional investors have consistently struggled to effectively monitor portfolio companies as stewards. In fact, to do so would run contrary to their nature. This nature therefore yields a maze of interest conflicts between institutional investors and true stewardship of portfolio companies. The

> short-term, comparative performance metrics upon which the vast majority of portfolio managers and funds are evaluated constrains institutional activism. 84 The performance of managers and funds is often monitored on a quarterly basis compared to similar funds or an index. This pervasive method of measuring performance does not easily accommodate long-term dialogue, even though it may potentially benefit individual shareholders in the long run.[37]

There can be a number of reasons for this 'reticence', including the free-rider principle—whereby one's competitors will benefit for free off of something that one absorbs the costs for. Yet, perhaps the most important issue affecting this so-called reticence is the time horizons that are applied. Why does the sector have such an issue with 'short-termism'?

The reasons for short-termism are many. Whist we will often hear that 'institutional investors' focus too much on the short-term, the variety within that definition makes such a generalisation complicated and likely unfair. There may be reasons for short-termism. One is that a manager's performance needs to be measured, and those who instruct a manager are usually sitting in a position of trust and mass responsibility to a lot of people. Let us go very simple for a moment. Let us say that I am an employee and as part of my salary I place some of my earnings into a pension fund. I am not financially savvy and pay little interest in financial concerns other than reading the reports that my pension fund send to me as a saver. It is not unreasonable to suggest that I want to know that the value of my savings are increasing and at the time of being able to draw my pension, that pot will be in a healthy shape. Those in charge of my pension fund, who will likely have instructed an asset manager to invest the contents of the pension fund in order to increase its value, now have to explain to me that the manager they have hired is doing a good job. The (very crude) theory goes that shorter-term performance can be measured, usually illustrated, and that is how performance and efficacy is *signalled* throughout the chain, especially when the 'unsophisticated' are involved with the financial marketplace. Admittedly that is all very crude and generalised, but the core concept of differing levels of sophistication, access to information, and ultimately care is all crucial to developing the building blocks of the financial culture that exists in most economies. In essence, it all comes down to one's ability to *signal*.

In addition, it is easier to discipline via short-termism, as the parameters are made clearer than they would be if longer-term thinking was employed. If an asset manager fails to hit particular metrics, say, for two quarters running, then it is clear they are in trouble. An asset owner can compare that performance with others, over the same timescale, and take relevant action if they deem it necessary to do so. If an entity then 'walks' i.e. severs a relationship or, in the case of an investor, divests from their position, the theory goes that such an action sends a signal of displeasure which adjoins to the threat of others 'walking' too, which clearly is not optimal. This is all very cost-efficient, according to the 'market for corporate control' theory.[38]

So, it may sound like we are saying short-termism works and long-termism does not. If that was the case, this book would not have been written because there would not have been the need to create a Stewardship Code in the first place; short-termism will only ever work in the short-term. The Financial Crisis was a clear example of what happens when the short-termism culture takes hold *too much*. To be cost effective is clearly a positive for the relevant industries and the economic theories that underpin them, but the remarkable social impact that such a culture had cannot be forgotten. So no, we are not saying short-termism works. What we are saying is that the new regulatory framework that is slowly being developed needs to consider the *actual* and not the *desired*. As Noguera said regarding the first two Codes:

> Overall, in developing the [Stewardship Code], the FRC failed to take account of present market and investment practices, exposing the [Stewardship Code's] shortcomings, and consequently minimising its impact.[39]

Everything is in place so that another opportunity is not missed. A new regulator, new political backing, and a further-increased general support of the concept of business doing better. This is not a rushed post-Crisis initiative anymore. Market practices need to be recognised and accepted first, before they can be changed. Then, there *must* be an incentive put in place. What that may be needs to be decided in conjunction with the market. The inclusion of more focus on ESG and particularly climate, is positive, but if it is, as it appears, majoritively based on the prerogative of the Government who is threatening hard law if it does not get what it wants, then the question of effective incentive is up for debate. Threat may encourage compliance, but it is questionable as to the real amount of buy-in one can illicit via threat. Does threat inspire one to not only comply, but also push the boundaries positively? We think not. However, the opposing argument may be that the market is consistently showing that it will not, as a market, push the boundaries itself so a threat-induced compliance may be the greater of the two when everything is considered. It is massively likely that the new regulator will find itself placed right in the middle of this conceptual tussle.

5.6 Conclusion

The future of stewardship, particularly in the UK, can go either way. On the one hand there is a fantastic opportunity to finally build a purpose-built infrastructure to allow for the concept of good stewardship to not only be complied with, but engrained within modern investment practice. Champions can be held-up as leading the pack. The benefits of a more engaged and longer-term thinking investment industry can become the real driving force for corporate change in the UK.

However, it can go the other way too. The move away from pushing for engagement points to a defeat for the regulator. That regulator, in a move which will not be lost on the marketplace, is being disbanded. The Government who disbanded it are ramping up the hard-law rhetoric with no evidence of hard law being appropriate or having the potential to be successful. In addition, this is a Government who is besieged with the need to make the decision to leave the European Union an economically, at least, successful one. The new regulator will have more powers than the FRC ever did, but with the environment being as it is at the time of its inception, one wonders whether it is hindered before it is born.

Irrespective, there are a number of crucial steps that need to be considered. The fundamental concepts of the constraints of one's fiduciary duty, and the importance and impact of real assurance, need to be truly understood and applied by the wider financial system. The issues associated with these elements, amongst many, need to be resolved before progress can be realised. We saw that there are potential issues with the concept of external assurance, but with a carefully considered regulatory infrastructure the benefits of external assurance can be realised and applied to the field of stewardship reporting; this could give the field more authority than anything else. With regards to fiduciary duty, there needs to be a resolution regarding whether such claims are absolutely valid, or a red herring.

One aspect that has not been really considered in the literature is the concept of educating the (financially) uneducated. If it is the case that the unsophisticated financial entities at the start of the financial chain (savers, pension holders etc.) can only be communicated with in such basic terms, then could this be an avenue to pursue? Is it really the case that a saver/pensioner who receives am annual report from their institutional investor would not understand the broadening of a time horizon if it was just explained honestly? Broadening a time horizon does not always, necessarily, increase one's risk. If it does, there can be countermeasures put in place to protect against that risk. It could even be the case that if that time horizon was broadened but for a particular purpose—maybe to invest in something more socially sustainable—then the broad consensus would be positive. There is a lot of assumption regarding what people will understand and accept, and that assumption is potentially being used for a cover-screen for approaches that may be easier, more cost-efficient, or even more traditional. In 2007/2008, it was that 'tradition' that brought the globe to its knees and we are still feeling that impact now. Perhaps some fundamental understandings need to change.

Notes

1. Financial Reporting Council, *The UK Stewardship Code 2020* (FRC 2020) https://www.frc.org.uk/getattachment/5aae591d-d9d3-4cf4-814a-d14e156a1d87/Stewardship-Code_Dec-19-Final-Corrected.pdf.
2. Financial Reporting Council, *Proposed Revision to the UK Stewardship Code* (2019) https://www.frc.org.uk/getattachment/8caa0e9c-58bb-41b2-923e-296223755174/Consultation-on-Proposed-Revisions-to-the-UK-Stewardship-Code-Jan-2019.pdf, 4 (2.2).
3. FCA/FRC, *Joint Consultation Feedback Statement* (2019) https://www.fca.org.uk/publications/feedback-statements/fs19-7-building-regulatory-framework-effective-stewardship, 4 (1.13).
4. FRC (n 2) 4 (2.2).
5. Paul L Davies, 'The UK Stewardship Code 2010–2010: From Saving the Company to Saving the Planet?' (2020) ECGI Working Paper Series 506/2020.
6. Law Commission, *Fiduciary Duties of Investment Intermediaries* (2014) https://s3-eu-west-2.amazonaws.com/lawcom-prod-storage-11jsxou24uy7q/uploads/2015/03/lc350_fiduciary_duties.pdf. The Law Commission did not recommend legislative reform but clarified the law: 'The primary concern of trustees must be to generate risk-adjusted returns. In doing so, they should take into account factors which are financially material to the performance of an investment. These may include environmental, social and governance factors' 6.100. On the Law Commission's

final report, see Susie Daykin, 'Pension Scheme Investment: Is it Always Just About the Money? To What Extent Can or Should Trustees Take Account of Ethical or ESG Factors when Investing? (2014) Travers Smith https://www.traverssmith.com/media/3255/susie_daykin__pension_scheme_investment_-_is_it_always____.pdf.

7. Anna Tilba and Arad Reisberg, 'Fiduciary Duty under the Microscope: Stewardship and the Spectrum of Pension Fund Engagement' (2019) 82 *Modern Law Review* 3, 456–87.
8. However, there is a growing number of studies confirming the effectiveness of engagement: Elroy Dimson, Oguzhan Karakas, and Xi Li, 'Active Ownership' 28 Review of Financial Studies 12; Andreas Hoepner, Ioannis Oikonomou, Zacharias Sautner, Laura T Starks, and Xiaoyan Zhou, 'ESH Shareholder Engagement and Downside Risk' (2020) ECGI Working Paper 671/2020.
9. Iris HY Chui, 'Stewardship as Investment Management for Institutional Shareholders' (2011) 32 *Company Lawyer* 3.
10. See, for example, Saker Nusseibeh, 'The Why Question' (2017) The 300 Club (March 6) https://www.the300club.org/blog/the-why-question/.
11. See Gordon L Clark, Andreas Feiner, and Michael Viehs, *From the Stockholder to the Stakeholder: How Sustainability Can Drive Financial Outperformance* (2015) https://arabesque.com/research/From_the_stockholder_to_the_stakeholder_web.pdf.
12. Benjamin J Richardson, 'Fossil Fuels Divestment: A Strategy for Sustainability?' in Clair Gammage and Tonia Novitz, *Sustainable Trade, Investment and Finance* (Edward Elgar 2019).
13. Ibid.
14. PRI, *Fiduciary Duty in the 21st Century: Final Report* (2019) https://www.unpri.org/download?ac=9792.
15. Ibid 23.
16. Roger Urwin, 'Pension Fund Fiduciary Duty and Its Impacts on Sustainable Investing' in James P. Hawley, Andreas G. F. Hoepner, Keith L. Johnson, Joakim Sandberg, and Edward J. Waitzer, *Cambridge Handbook of Institutional Investment and Fiduciary Duty* (Cambridge University Press 2014).
17. A relevant recent case in Australia was settled by the fund before a court hearing, see Adam Morton, 'Australian Super Fund Agrees to Factor Climate Crisis into Decisions in "Groundbreaking" Case' (2020) *The Guardian* (November 2) https://amp-theguardian-com.cdn.ampproject.org/c/s/amp.theguardian.com/australia-news/2020/nov/02/australian-super-fund-agrees-to-factor-climate-crisis-into-decisions-in-groundbreaking-case. As part of the settlement, the fund committed to more climate related disclosures, conduct scenario analysis to inform its

investment strategy and engage in advocacy with the objective for the companies it invests in to comply with the goals of the Paris agreement.

18. Law Commission, *Fiduciary Duties of Investment Intermediaries* (2014) https://s3-eu-west-2.amazonaws.com/lawcom-prod-storage-11jsxou24uy7q/uploads/2015/03/lc350_fiduciary_duties.pdf, 101.
19. Peter Montagnon, 'Good Stewardship Must Begin with Fiduciary Duty' (2019) *Financial Times* (March 11) https://www.ft.com/content/bc22cb56-ea97-3f8e-a963-c91a116fe555.
20. (n 7) 483.
21. Peter Carey, Arifur Khan, Dessalegn G Mihret, and Mohammad B Muttakin, 'Voluntary Sustainability Assurance, Capital Constraint and Cost of Debt: International Evidence' (2021) 25 *International Journal of Auditing* 2 367 351–73.
22. Geert Braam and Roy Peeters, 'Corporate Sustainability Performance and Assurance on Sustainability Reports: Diffusion of Accounting Practices in the Realm of Sustainable Development' (2018) 25 *Corporate Social Responsibility and Environmental Management* 178 164–81.
23. Anil Gurturk, *Integrated Reporting and Sustainability-Related Assurance: Current Practice and Future Directions* (Kassel University Press 2017) 62.
24. FRC, *Draft Strategy and Plan & Budget: 2021/22* (2021) https://www.frc.org.uk/getattachment/7180cf28-aa17-4a2a-9f8c-f737af8032be/FRC-Draft-Strategy-and-Plan-Budget-February-2021.pdf.
25. Braam and Peeters (n 22) 167.
26. Ibid.
27. Nonna Martinov-Bennie, Geoff Frost and Dominic SB Soh, 'Assurance on Sustainability Reporting: State of Play and Future Directions' in Stewart Jones and Janek Ratnatunga, *Contemporary Issues in Sustainability Accounting, Assurance and Reporting* (Emerald 2012) 268.
28. Gurturk (n 23) 88.
29. Charika Channuntapitat, 'Can Sustainability Report Assurance Be a Collaborative Process and Practice Beyond the Ritual of Verification?' 30 *Business Strategy and the Environment* 2 775 775–86.
30. Julie Matheson and Lucinda Soon, 'The Long and Winding Road… That Leads to… ARGA' (2021) Lexology (February 19) https://www.lexology.com/library/detail.aspx?g=49bbe546-c5d9-439a-9452-16cd66a0e331.
31. Financial Reporting Council, 'Update on the FRC Transformation Programme' (2020) https://www.frc.org.uk/news/may/update-on-frc-s-transformation-programme.
32. Julie Matheson and Lucinda Soon, 'The Long and Winding Road… That Leads to… ARGA' (2021) Lexology (February 19) https://www.lexology.com/library/detail.aspx?g=49bbe546-c5d9-439a-9452-16cd66a0e331.

33. Department for Business, Energy and Industrial Strategy (BEIS), *Restoring Trust in Audit and Corporate Governance: Consultation on the Government's Proposals* (March 2021) https://assets.publishing.service.gov.uk/government/uploads/system/uploads/attachment_data/file/970673/restoring-trust-in-audit-and-corporate-governance-command-paper.pdf 206.
34. Ibid.
35. Ibid 207.
36. Khalid Azizuddin, 'Danish Regulator Sets Up Enforcement Unit for SFDR and Greenwashing' (2021) Responsible Investor (March 14) https://www.responsible-investor.com/articles/danish-regulator-sets-up-enforcement-unit-for-sfdr-and-greenwashing.
37. David W. Roberts, 'Agreement in Principle: A Compromise for Activist Shareholders from the UK Stewardship Code' (2015) 48 *Vanderbilt Journal of Transnational Law* 2 556 543–76.
38. James Noguera, 'Institutional Investors and the Stewardship Code: An Analysis of Why Institutional Investors Do Not Monitor or Engage' (2017) 28 *International Company and Commercial Law Review* 3 108 107–14.
39. Ibid 107.

CHAPTER 6

Conclusion

> One consequence of a more dispersed and disinterested ownership structure is that it becomes harder to exert influence over management, increasing the risk of suboptimal decision-making. There is some empirical support for this hypothesis. For example, companies tend to have higher valuations when institutional shareholders are a large share of cash flow, perhaps reflecting their stewardship role in protecting the firm from excessive risk-taking.[1]

Stewardship, as we now know, is not a modern concept. However, in applying it to the concept of an institutional investor in order to encourage the increase in their role within the governance of corporations, stewardship has taken on a new energy. The modern development of an institutional investor-dominated marketplace has led to some fundamental reconsiderations of traditional economic thought. The parameters set forth by Berle and Means in the 1930s do not, necessarily, apply any more. The forces that influence a sole shareholder, a person who may hold shares just in one company, simply do not apply to the modern institutional investor, who may hold thousands of shares in thousands of companies.

In that sense, and particularly as a consequence of the era-defining Financial Crisis, it is absolutely right to re-assess the framework surrounding 'the investor'. The need to reconsider the modern investor landscape was known and articulated well before the Financial Crisis, but

D. Cash and R. Goddard, *Investor Stewardship and the UK Stewardship Code*, https://doi.org/10.1007/978-3-030-87152-9_6

with focus elsewhere (like on the direct governance of the company from its organisational structure), it was not until the aftermath of the Financial Crisis that the world saw its first, State-supported *Stewardship Code*. On paper in black and white, it looks monumental. It looks like the turning of a page, the beginning of a new paradigm within the financial sector. In reality, it was not close. It was the re-purposing of a decades-old voluntary Code that many were already following and surpassing. Yet, the scene had been set for something to be done.

As the 2010s rumbled on the financial sector transitioned between crises, there were calls for something better to be done. To answer those calls, the new *UK Stewardship Code 2020* was developed. This Code, instead of hastily just calling for more engagement without ever really considering the constitution, nature, and culture of the investors it was aiming itself at, now asks for something different from the marketplace. It asks it to take responsibility. It asks it to take responsibility not only for itself, but for society. Crucially, species-defining concerns like climate change are now being pushed onto private investors. This can have only one of two outcomes: either the idea to summon and guide private interests to resolving something which modern business is directly contributing to is an inspired one, or it is not. If it is, there is a real opportunity to push through societal benefits like that which has never been seen before. The impact of modern business upon the global society can be demonstrably reduced and transformed into an inherently positive one. However, if this fails, the impact could be lasting.

We have seen in this book that there is a widely held sentiment that it is now or never for the concept of a *Stewardship Code*. Even the British Government are raising the stakes, threatening non-compliance with hard law which fundamentally changes the nature of the relationship between investors and society, and also arguably affects, absolutely, the chances of meaningful success in this area (although that can of course be debated!) Worse still, there exists the chance that there will be a middle-ground whereby the concept of stewardship is continued and supported, but society does not gain from it. If we see evidence of more box-ticking, more 'boilerplate' reporting, and if external assurance services become mainstream and we see the growth of conflicted services, then the ultimate impact upon society can be massively but negatively impactful. There can be no room for corruptive practices in the modern development of investor stewardship.

Yet, we remain hopeful. The opening quote to this conclusion, from Mr Andrew Haldane (the former Chief Economist for the Bank of England) portrays a belief that the inclusion and participation of institutional investor in the modern corporate arena is a positive for the value of the company. Evidence can be found for this. It is now the chance to show that the participation of institutional investors in the modern corporate arena can be more than that; it can be *societally valuable* too. The will to do good in the investor community is visible and palpable. It is just the case, we argue, that there are systemic misalignments that need to be rectified if success is to be achieved. Investors need to do more in terms of pushing the boundaries. Regulators need to do more in terms of pushing for resolutions to the issues surround fiduciary duties and the development of genuine assurance services. There needs to be much more education for those whose investments/savings/pension contributions start this whole process. The concept of long-termism and societally beneficial financial practice needs to be cherished, protected, and championed at all costs. It cannot be 'co-opted' for political gain. It cannot be displaced because of a lack of resources for this regulator or that regulator. It is an *ideal* and an ideal can break through any boundary. However, with the new Code, the new Regulator, and the remarkably volatile environment within which we all live, we are now in a time were that ideal will be massively tested. The results of rising to that challenge, or being defeated by it, will be laid out for us all to see, and sooner than most of us would like to admit.

However, there is a larger question which we have only hinted at throughout the book: is the concept of a Stewardship Code, in itself, a sign of success or failure? Why does the marketplace even need a Stewardship Code? It could be argued that the existence of a Stewardship Code is a sign of abstract failure in the marketplace, and that it is merely a temporary stop-gap plugging a hole in a dam. What that stop-gap does not do is address defects in the dam's structural fortitude. Whilst the new Code is an upgrade on the previous Codes, is it just a bigger stop-gap? What it certainly is, conceptually, is a determination in the pathway that has been chosen. Rather than ask the question of why private institutional investors cannot be trusted to act in a way that does not preserve the world around them, the 'system' has endeavoured to encourage them to do so. One wonders whether the existence of, and need for a Stewardship Code reveals the answer that encouraging the market participants to act as better stewards means, fundamentally, one can never achieve that outcome.

Note

1. Jennifer G Hill, 'Good Activist/Bad Activist: The Rise of International Stewardship Codes' (2018) 41 *Seattle University Law Review* 2 497–524, 504.

Index

A

Asset manager, 2, 20, 21, 23, 24, 28, 39, 40, 43, 45, 47, 48, 55–57, 60, 65–67

Asset owner, 2, 20, 21, 23–25, 39, 40, 43, 45–47, 55–57, 60, 65, 67

Assurance, 40, 45, 46, 49, 54, 58–62, 68, 74, 75

Audit, Reporting Governance Authority (ARGA), 27, 37, 50, 53, 54, 60, 62, 64, 71

C

Cadbury Report, 7, 8

Cadbury, Sir Adrian, 1, 7

D

Diversification, 7, 14, 21

E

Environmental, Social, and Governance (ESG), 13, 22, 24, 31, 33, 40, 41, 43–47, 49, 50, 55–59, 67, 69

F

Fiduciary duty(ies), 20–22, 30, 32, 46, 54–57, 61, 68, 75

Financial Reporting Council (FRC), 10–15, 19, 20, 25–27, 29, 31, 34, 37–40, 42–45, 47–51, 53, 54, 58, 62–65, 67–69

Freshfields Bruckhaus Deringer, 22, 33

H

Hempel Report, 8

Hempel, Sir Ronald, 8

I

Institute of Chartered Accountants in England and Wales (ICAEW), 26, 27, 34

Institutional Shareholders Committee (ISC), 7

D. Cash and R. Goddard, *Investor Stewardship and the UK Stewardship Code*, https://doi.org/10.1007/978-3-030-87152-9

Investment mandate, 2, 8, 23, 24
Investor capitalism, 3
ISC Code, 10–13

K
Kingman Review, 25, 31, 37, 62

L
Law Commission, 22, 32, 55, 58, 69, 71

N
Net-zero carbon, 39
Nonfinancial, 22, 23, 50, 55, 56, 58–62

P
Paris Climate Accord, 39

S
Shareholders Rights Directive II (SRD II), 29, 30

T
Treasury Select Committee, 6

U
United National Environment Programme (UNEP), 22, 33

W
Walker Report, 7
Walker, Sir David, 7, 9

The manufacturer's authorised representative in the EU is Springer Nature Customer Service Centre GmbH, Europaplatz 3, 69115 Heidelberg, Germany. If you have any concerns regarding our products, please contact ProductSafety@springernature.com

Printed and bound by CPI Group (UK) Ltd, Croydon, CR0 4YY
30/09/2026
02225514-0001